Unwin Education Books: 21

BEYOND CONTROL?

Unwin Education Books

Series Editor: Ivor Morrish, BD, BA, Dip. Ed. (London), BA (Bristol)

Unwin Education Books: 21
Series Editor: Ivor Morrish

Beyond Control?
a study of discipline
in the comprehensive school

PAUL FRANCIS

London   George Allen & Unwin
Ruskin House   Museum Street

First published in 1975

© George Allen & Unwin Ltd 1975

ISBN 0 04 371033 6 hardback
     0 04 371034 4 paperback

Printed in Great Britain
in 10 point Times Roman
by Clarke, Doble & Brendon Ltd
Plymouth

To 3B4/5,
with whom,
and therefore for whom,
I could do nothing

Acknowledgements

My main debt is to the endless number of teachers, students and school pupils from whom I have learned something about teaching. The views expressed are very much my own but their origins are various, and I apologise for any unacknowledged borrowings which seem unduly blatant.

More particularly, I am grateful to those friends and former pupils who have given me their own accounts of situations in which they were personally involved. I am indebted also to those interested and long-suffering friends who have helped me explore these problems and clarify my ideas, whether in my car on the way to school, staff-room conversations or in numerous informal sessions in a variety of venues.

My last and greatest thanks must go to my wife, who gave me her loyalty and support, some help with typing, the benefit of brief but unerring criticism, and a generous share of the kitchen table.

1974   *Kilburn, Derbyshire*

Contents

References

I have referred to, or quoted from, the following books:

W. T. Davies and T. B. Shepherd, *Teaching; Begin Here* (Epworth, 1949; rev. edn, 1961)

R. Farley, *Secondary Modern Discipline* (Black, 1960)

B. Hines, *Kestrel for a Knave* (Michael Joseph, Penguin, 1968)

D. H. Lawrence, *The Rainbow* (Heinemann, 1915, and Penguin, 1973)

L. F. Loewenstein, *Violence in Schools and Its Treatment* (NAS, 1972)

A. S. Neill, *Talking about Summerhill* (Gollancz, 1967)

P. Newell, *A Last Resort?* (Penguin, 1972)

N. Otty, *Learner Teacher* (Penguin, 1972)

R. S. Peters, *Ethics and Education* (Allen & Unwin, 1966)

J. Rowan, *The Writing on the Blackboard* (Stacey, 1973)

Turner (ed.), *Discipline in Schools* (Ward Lock, 1973)

I have also quoted from *Libertarian Education No. 11* (Lib.Ed. group, 180 Melbourne Road, Leicester).

At other points I have either referred to specific teachers and pupils, or quoted from writings which they have given me, in the knowledge that these might be published. In all cases, names have been either omitted or changed.

Bibliography

The purpose of a bibliography is either to demonstrate the erudition of the author, or to indicate to the reader how he may best pursue a line of inquiry. In my own case, this book reflects experience rather than study, and I have no wish to direct anyone to further reading. The next step, in my view, is practical and communal: criticism, observation, discussion and action.

Introduction

This book is about discipline in comprehensive schools. By 'discipline' I mean what most teachers mean, a class-room of thirty kids with a teacher in charge of them, exercising or seeking some form of control. This may not be an inspiring, creative or permanent situation, but it is one in which many of us spend much of our time, and for that reason student teachers ought to know about it.

I confine myself to comprehensive schools because they are the schools within which I have taught, because they currently attract intense attention, and because they will increasingly be the pattern of our secondary education. That is not to say, however, that none of what follows will be relevant to teachers in independent, grammar or primary schools. Nor do I claim exhaustive experience of the extensive variety of comprehensives; there are many schools rougher than the two in which I have taught, as well as many teachers whose control and understanding exceed my own. Unfortunately, most of these teachers are too busy or too exhausted to write books.

My immediate purpose is to look at the disciplinary problems which face young teachers, and to offer some short-term answers as a guide to survival. This may seem a cynical, limited objective, but it does at least take seriously the anxiety and misery currently experienced by many students and probationers. It is my optimistic faith that such suffering can be alleviated through a rational study of some present difficulties and available solutions.

This is not an area which encourages experts. Discipline is a highly subjective and controversial topic, and no orthodox academic qualification recognises understanding of or achievements in the control of school classes. Paradoxically, those most instantly successful in the process of exacting obedience from school pupils often know little about it, since their automatic exercise of power saves them the trouble of ever having to think about it.

The best qualifications for writing such a book, therefore, may be typical rather than exceptional. I started teaching in a comprehensive school six years ago, keen, innocent and apparently well qualified. By the end of my first year I had three classes which I had to lose for their sakes as well as my own, and was in danger of failing my probationary year. Now, I am still teaching in comprehensive schools and manage to control most of my classes most of the time, but I still encounter kids who do not immediately do as I ask. I am experienced enough to have a clearer idea of what I am trying to do and how I seek to do it, but I am not so eminent as to have forsaken teaching kids for administration or educational theory.

At a time when the confidence of public pronouncements about school discipline is in direct proportion to the speaker's distance from the class-room, it seems to me urgent that practising class teachers make some contribution to the debate, through formal publication as well as through the fragmentary, local discussions which already take place. Part of the value of this book, in my view, will lie in its very limitations, in that it has been written by a teacher, about his own work, during evenings, weekends and holidays. Without the benefit of empirical research or secondment, I have tried to produce one teacher's picture of the class-room, a picture which has had to be squeezed in between marking, preparation and sleep, as well as one which has changed with each crisis, confrontation and staff-room chat.

In the short term, so immediate a view must be both individual and practical, and the core of this book is simply a personal offer of conversation to young teachers, indicating ways in which I think they might save themselves some grief. The extent to which that advice is either relevant or helpful must be, of course, for the individual reader to decide.

We do not, however, work in a vacuum, and in the area of school discipline there is an urgent general need to relate theory and action, philosophy and practice. *Beyond Control?* thus seeks to raise questions as well as to propose solutions, and so combat the consensus of embarrassment within the educational orthodoxy which has for so long left young teachers ignorant and unprepared. Parts One and Three are intended as an initial remedy for our past failure to discuss discipline with honesty and realism. In those sections I seek to stimulate a closer and more radical questioning of the way we run our schools, which should involve practising teachers and parents as well as educationalists and students.

A full-length study of discipline, therefore, need not be an endorsement of the *status quo*. On the contrary, if we wish to effect intelligent change, we need first of all to look carefully and fully at the way things are; with discipline, we need to look at the arguments for control and the means through which it may be achieved before we can hope to pass beyond them.

Prologue

Out of Control

The bell went.

Six lessons gone, he thought, and one round to go, as 1C swept deliriously out to claim their break. Tony Jenkins stepped back to avoid being crushed, and watched indulgently as his liberated charges chattered, jostled and were gone.

He sat down and surveyed the debris. Bells might be an impersonal restriction, but they certainly got rid of kids very efficiently. It hadn't been bad, all things considered. A bit wild in parts, but if you're asking kids to say what they think it's bound to make a bit of a racket, and at least you can be sure they're alive. It annoyed him that they wouldn't listen to each other, but they were young and keen to talk, and they had plenty of time to learn the subtler etiquette of conversation. A pity he'd forgotten to set homework, but it didn't really matter; they'd probably appreciate an evening free while the summer weather still lasted.

Tony wandered round the room, straightening out chairs and picking up the largest bits of paper – where on earth did it all come from? In the first week he'd gone down to the staff-room for a cup of tea at break, but now he didn't bother; by the time he'd got there he'd found a long queue and nowhere to sit, so he'd spent afternoon breaks for the last two weeks in his teaching room, losing a cup of tea but gaining a moment of peace, and the chance to think about the last double of the day. Today was Friday, which meant 4Z, and 4Z needed thinking about.

On interview, when the head had said 'We'd require you, Mr Jenkins, to teach the full ability range', Tony had nodded brightly, without a trace of snobbery or fear. Now, he had more clue of what that meant, although he wasn't at all sure how he was going to cope – education department lectures didn't look as though they were going to be very relevant to 4Z on a Friday afternoon. Still, he wanted to try, and he'd hardly started yet.

'What we doing, sir?' Ronnie, a scruffy little youth with angelic eyes and a perpetual twitch, had wandered in without his noticing. The question was academic, as Ronnie couldn't sit still for five minutes and hadn't brought a pen to English lessons yet, but it was nice of him to ask.

'Oh, a bit of everything,' Tony stalled. He went back over last night's preparation – if you could call it that. After a shattering week and a couple of pints it had seemed enough to write '4Z: plays, Friend stories, reader' but now he wasn't so sure. Anyway, that Mrs Courtman said she planned as she walked through the door, and she didn't seem to be anything special.

The bell saved him from worrying any further. Break was over, and rounds seven and eight under way. Over the next five minutes 4Z spilled into the room, favourite places were claimed with shouts and occasional shoves, and Tony Jenkins watched with amused detachment as the pecking order asserted itself. They had all been streamed, but that didn't make them all the same. Some were more equal than others, but most ended up with a chair.

'Please, sir?' Timid inquiry from scruffy, earnest Jenny.

'Yes?'

'Ey, sir!' boomed Terry from the back, grinning strangely.

'What?'

'Who's your favourite pupil?'

He meant Barry, but Tony couldn't afford to show that he knew that. He had noticed Barry's absence, and was praying it was permanent.

'I don't have favourites,' he said piously.

'Get away. He's away, anyway. Said he can't come.'

'Yeah, Barry's helping his grandad', Ted volunteered, and he too had a smile spreading over his beaming face. Inwardly, Tony congratulated himself on his luck, and maintained a cool, impassive façade – he hoped.

'Sir?'

'Yes, Jenny?'

'Please, sir, Norma's in my place, sir.'

'No, I ain't.' Norma, hard as nails and twice as spiky, clearly wasn't in the mood to move. Mr Jenkins chose discretion.

'Yes, well . . . there's a place over there.'

'She's not coming here!' scandalised yell from Ken, whose mates found it briefly funny, and threw in congratulations, whistles and obscene suggestions.

'She's not sitting wi' us, sir.'

'But that's my place, sir, where Norma is.'

'Jenny, will you please sit down there.'

Quiet and uncomplaining, she went, as he'd known she would. Perhaps, travelling round for eight lessons a day with Norma Lewis, you got used to giving in. Still, ten minutes gone and nothing happening, except two girls reading a pop magazine and Ronnie wandering round the room trying to pick a fight. Well, it could have been worse; they all had a place and at least Barry Edwards was away.

'Right, we'll start now.'

'What?'

'What did he say?'

'What we doing, sir?'

'I'm just going to tell you.'

'You what?'

'Shut up!'

There were times when the incessant questions drove him mad. It wasn't as if they'd got anything to say either, but still they chattered on. For the moment, though, raising his voice had stilled them, and he relished the pause before going on.

'First, I want to finish the plays we were doing yesterday and. . . .' He stopped as the eyes stopped watching him. The crash from the door announced the arrival of Barry Edwards, who, having made his effect, surveyed the room coolly.

'Afternoon.'

'I beg your pardon?'

'Don't mention it, Mr Jerkins . . . I mean Jenkins.' Terry, Ted and Bill, pleased with their little stratagem and delighted with their leader's entry, broke into whistling applause. This was too much.

'Get out, Edwards.'

'Suit yourself.' Calmly, Barry winked at his mates, turned and began walking down the corridor, whistling. Tony knew, with horrible certainty, that he couldn't let him go. Mr Archer might be prowling around, and anyway Barry would only go outside and make faces through the window as he'd done last Tuesday.

'Come back.' Tony walked briskly, breathlessly out of the door to find Barry, master of the situation, coolly waiting for him.

'Make up your mind, *sir*.'

'Where have you been?'

'Seein' the headmaster. Ask him if you don't believe me.'

It was likely enough. Anyway, there was no way of checking and the lesson hadn't started yet. From the room came isolated feminine squeals and a half-hearted chorus of 'Jerky, Jerky' which he thought was Ted and Terry.

'All right, Edwards, come in and sit down.'

As Barry sauntered in and found himself a corner chair with casual ease, Tony noticed Norma painting her nails, little Ronnie idly kicking his legs against the side wall, and the two girls whose names he could never remember still looking at their magazine. Time for action.

'Right now, 4Z. Quiet please.'

The chatter went on. The two girls looked up from *Pop Interview* No. 235, stared at him blankly, and then carried on reading.

'Stop that. Now listen', he said, louder.

'Shut up, can't you see he's trying to say something', said Alice, fiercely prim, even in the jungle of 4Z.

'Yes, miss', mimicked Ken, to a chorus of cheers and ridicule.

'Stop that, all of you. Now will you please listen.'

As the chatter continued Tony wondered, insanely analytical, why he bothered with that 'please'. He was about to shout again when a piercing whistle split the room, stopped at least four separate conversations and made the two girls look up.

'Who was that?' Tony asked, quite unnecessarily.

Barry answered, genuinely aggrieved, 'I did you a favour.'

'Get out.'

He stared back sullenly.

'I said, get out.'

'You wanted them shut up. I shut them up.'

'Yeah, he was helpin' you, sir', from Terry.

'Just 'cos you couldn't do it yerself', from someone.

'Shut up and *get out*!'

A real shout, this, not simply a raising of the voice, and for the moment it seemed to be enough. Keeping his dignity, barging slowly past his mates, Barry edged his way out of the room.

'Keep your hair on, Jerky', he muttered as he went.

Tony ignored him. He had the rest to worry about, and if Barry Edwards wanted to waste time with childish nicknames that was up to him; he wasn't going to give him the satisfaction of getting drawn in. Besides, he'd seen too many teachers obsessed with their own dignity and position and he wasn't going to end up like them. It wasn't the bowing and scraping that mattered, but the teaching. With Edwards gone, he had a chance. 'Right, now we'll do the plays. Ken, your group.'

Tony watched, relieved, as they cleared a space, built up a huge wall of tables and desks and whispered furiously about who was meant to be doing what. He wondered why it took so long for any of them to get anything moving; at first it hadn't been so bad, but in a mere three weeks they'd got worse rather than better.

The boys, having cleared a space and announced who they were, acted their 'play', a prolonged fight about three men asking a stranger for a light and then beating him up in a sidestreet – hence the factory wall.

'You didn't say much', said Tony.

'You don't when you're beating someone up', Ronnie replied.

'But you're supposed to talk in plays.'

'So?'

'Why? Who says you have to talk? Who wants to talk?' asked Phil, hurt by the coolness of their reception. Tony Jenkins laughed at this novel theory of drama, and asked 'Well, d'you want to do mime?' but got only a blank stare by way of reply.

'Right. Norma, your group.'

'Margaret won't do it.'

'She's got to, hasn't she, sir?'

'If she's not doing it, I'm not.'

'What's the matter, scared?'

'Why should she?'

'We did a play – you've got to do one.'

'Call that a play? Just a lot of fighting.'

'Great!' said Ronnie, who'd been in it.

Tony watched, amazed by their capacity to conjure a war out of nothing. He didn't want a row, but something would have to happen soon. Ken and his gang, their performance finished, were sitting in a huddle, throwing occasional insults at the girls but becoming increasingly concerned with something else. Tony had only just seen the cards when he knew by the sudden stillness that a visitor had arrived. The class rose to their feet.

'So sorry to interrupt, Mr Jenkins.'

Was he joking? You could never tell with Archer. Best to bluff, anyway.

'That's quite all right, Mr Archer.'

'I found this young man loitering in a corridor. I understand that he's with you.'

Tony turned to face a barely recognisable Barry Edwards, standing outside without a trace of swagger.

'Um . . . er . . . yes.' Archer was still staring at him, half politely. Some further explanation seemed to be called for.

'He whistled, sir.'

'Whistled?'

It sounded stupid, put like that, but there wasn't anything else to say.
'I see. Well, you shouldn't be whistling in lessons, should you, boy?'
'No, sir.'
'No, sir. Well, as long as you understand that, I'm sure Mr Jenkins
will allow you to return to his lesson.'
'Er . . . yes. Um . . . of course.'
He fought down a desire to refuse, an urge to plead with Mr Archer
to take Barry Edwards, and the whole of stinking 4Z come to that,
and drop them down some large hole where he need never see them
again. He said nothing. Even if he did only teach two sixth-form
lessons a week, Mr Archer remained headmaster, and that was that.
Headmasterly, he looked round now at the pop magazine, the wall
of desks and the playing cards, stared straight at Tony for what felt
like a full minute, and then left.
In the moment of silence which followed his departure Tony acted.
He told them to straighten their chairs and get out their books; he
cursed himself for not thinking of it sooner – if in doubt, get them
writing, that's what they said. There were groans, banging of desk
lids and a few complaints about plays unperformed, but enough of
Mr Archer's aura hung in the air for the transition to be relatively
painless.
'Now I want you to. . . .'
'Got a pen, sir?'
'You've got my book, sir.'
'Shut up.'
'Cor, ratty, ain't he?'
'I said shut up!'
He knew that if he carried on shouting he'd rupture his throat by
4.00 p.m., and they were barely half way there yet. Taking a breath
he tried to do it all in one, gabbling:
'I want a story in your books about something you did with a
friend.'
'Can it be a girl friend?' from Barry.
'Yes.' Just like they had told him in lectures, 'Children can often
use language as a means of exploring their own emotional experience.'
'Can it be about . . . you know, sir?'
'No, I don't know. What?'
'*Sex!*' came the shout, powerful but anonymous. Dirty laughs, and
dirtier gestures, from the boys. Ted drew something on a blank piece
of paper and passed it to Andy, who was soon scribbling busily. Not
much exploration there.
'Anything you like', said Tony wearily, to more cheers.

'Please, sir, have you got my book, sir?'

Jenny again, and she was right, dammit. He'd been marking it that morning. Now, where the hell had he put it?

'Mine too, sir.' From Ronnie.

'I haven't got yours', said Tony, bluffing.

'Nor have I', said Ronnie, with an honest face, also bluffing.

'Look for it, then.'

'I have, sir.'

'Oh, do it on paper.'

He turned round, desperate for paper, anything he could lay his hands on. Finding a new book, he ripped two pages out of the middle before he realised it bore the name of one of his first-year girls. Still, she'd never know.

'There you are. Now, get on with it.' Ronnie and Jenny departed to play and work respectively, and Tony, exhausted, looked at his watch.

'What we meant to be doing, sir?'

'Got a pen?'

'What date is it?'

'Anyone got a pen?'

'Sir, how d'you spell "immediately"?'

'Shut up!'

He walked angrily to the board and had just written 'My Friend' when a paper dart flew across the room and slid neatly under his desk, to the accompaniment of a high-pitched laugh. Andy Fairweather, it must be.

'Fairweather.' A shout of surprised laughter told him he'd picked the wrong one.

'Sir?'

'Pick up that dart.'

'It wasn't me, sir.'

'I said, pick it up.'

'Blimey, it's a prison camp, this is, not a school.' He walked down to the front, picked up the dart and dropped it in the bin, and returned to his place near the back, pausing only to tip up the chair on which Ronnie was precariously balanced. For the thousandth time in his life he fell over.

Tony, who liked Ronnie and couldn't help finding him funny, was past caring. By now title and date were on the board, plus a list of questions they had to answer.

'That's all you need. I want a page from each of you or you'll do it for homework. Now get on with it.'

The 'please' had vanished; it was a battle of wills and he was going to get something out of them, even if it was only a few illegible lines scribbled under duress.

'I can't do a page', from Ronnie.

'Well, you'll just have to try, won't you?' He was surprised by the toughness of his own reply, and wondered if he'd be a staff-room cynic by the time he was 40, barking at kids like that bloke in physics. Was it going to be like this all the time? 4Z, for five lessons a week, three terms a year, for thirty years? Tony surfaced from his gloomy meditation to see that rarity, a patient, raised hand. Percy, a slow, solemn lad with great round eyes, was looking at him.

'Please, sir?'

'Yes, Percy?'

'What do I do next?'

Tony walked across to Percy's desk in the front row, and looked at his book. As English, it didn't begin to exist. Like inky worms the line snaked across the page, blots and squiggles decorating the margin. Tony, intrigued by this new code, fetched his chair and placed it next to Percy's desk. He asked Percy to read what he'd written so far, which he did, laboriously, line by line. Tony tried to make him see where he paused, where the full stops ought to be, but Percy, though willing, had never got on with full stops. Refusing to despair, and enjoying the personal contact, Tony went on to talk about how the story would develop, asking what was going to happen next. Awkwardly, but with growing confidence, Percy began to explain.

Bang. Out of the relative calm, an explosion.

'What was that?'

'Who did it?'

'Ey up, Barry!'

'What d'you mean – wasn't me.'

A crisp bag, empty and split for ever, lay prominently on the floor in front of the back row of desks. Probably Barry, but as Tony saw the cold, challenging stare he knew it was useless to accuse without evidence. Still, he had been getting somewhere with Percy, and he wasn't just going to give in; they'd got away with a lot, but they weren't going to get away with this.

'Well, who was responsible for that?'

The grins went down the line. He noticed Graham sitting the other side of Ken, where there hadn't been a chair before. And surely that little fair one, Ernie or Eric or something, hadn't he been at the front? What was he doing in the back row, grinning?

'I'm waiting . . . well, who was it?'

A bored contemptuous silence, interrupted only by the occasional scrape of a chair leg or 'plop' as Ronnie discovered, yet again, that his finger and cheek could co-operate to make a noise.

'Very well, you'll all stay in at 4 o'clock.'

Outcry.

'I'm not stayin' in.'

'My bus goes at 4.30.'

'We've got a match tonight.'

'Yeah, so've we.'

'It wasn't me.'

'What do we have to stay for?'

'*Shut up*! The next person who talks 'll get a detention.'

'Blimey!' from Ken, loudly.

'Detention!' yelled Andy Fairweather.

'You're both in detention', Tony countered; determined, having made his threat, to keep it.

'See you in doghouse, Ken.'

'Yeah. I'm in all next week, anyway.'

'He can't put me in, my bus goes at 4.'

'Oh, aren't they rude!' from an exasperated Alice. Tony sighed inwardly, knowing what was coming. Gleefully, Andy seized his chance.

'She was talking, sir. She's got to have one.'

'No, I haven't.' No one had ever dreamed of putting Alice in detention before; shaken, she looked to Tony for reassurance.

'Right, I'll see Ken, Andy . . . and, er, Alice at the end of the lesson. The rest of you, pack up your exercise books . . . no, on second thoughts perhaps it'd be better if you handed them in.'

Shouts of relief; any movement, any decision, brought 4 o'clock that bit closer, and though they didn't know there were still fifteen minutes to go, it was clear that this teacher wouldn't be wanting anything else from them. He looked round the room, at the shambles. A mere eight books on a desk at the front, with three more on the floor and others God knows where; Ronnie ambling round in a world of his own, the boys talking among themselves and Norma, contemptuous and aloof, combing her hair. Alice, bitter and tearful, was whispering vehemently to her friend. What a time to start a story.

'What we doing?' from Barry, almost polite in the certainty of eventual triumph.

'Bell's gone.' An old gambit, unconvincing, from Terry.

'The bell has not gone.'

'Hasn't it?'

'What we packed up for, then?'

'We're going to read another story from the reader.'

'Oh no.' A vast, communal groan. He had to admit, they had taste. For them, it was a ridiculous book; *Ten Modern Short Stories*, and so they had been fifty years ago, when aristocratic gentry had hours of leisure and vocabularies to match. Still, it had been the only set left. Tony bent down to the cupboard by the blackboard to fetch them, and nearly jumped at the deafening crash. He looked round and was relieved to see that it was only Ronnie, charming and indestructible.

'Fell off me chair, sir.'

'Where was it, on the ceiling?'

He could have bitten his tongue off. It wasn't a great joke, just a flip reaction under pressure. But they wouldn't let it go. Sir had made a joke, and was going to get a laugh, whether he wanted it or not. Between them the boys at the back made it last a good two minutes, leaning back, slapping each other, repeating the joke and then laughing again taking twice as much time as the original incident. Tony, the culprit, watched helplessly.

He was rescued by Phil, a quick eager kid who couldn't bear to do nothing. 'Shall I give 'em out?' he asked, indicating the pile of readers Tony had dropped on the floor.

'Er, yes . . . thank you, Phil.' Somebody might as well do something useful, Tony thought, even if he himself couldn't. He thought gloomily of the old men of the staff-room and the heartless post-mortems they held on Janice Hargreaves, the maths girl who had such trouble. Perhaps they'd talk about him now; perhaps they did already – there was no way of telling.

'What about us? Don't we get one?'

Norma's threatening question drew Tony back to the present. Phil had efficiently ensured that every boy in the class, except Percy, had a book. Tony thought that there'd been twenty or more, but the rest were nowhere to be seen.

'All right, all right, one between two.' At this rate there wouldn't be time to finish anyway, but you couldn't pack up in midstream. 'You should know from last time, someone'll have to share. Now, let's get started or we won't have time to finish it.'

As if he cared a toss. Still, he couldn't just sit there and stare at them for ten minutes, and he was meant to be a teacher. The books had not moved; no girl had a copy.

'Pass these books round, will you?' he yelled, furious at the pointless destructiveness of it all. Could they run the lesson any better, them sitting back there, grinning confidently at his unease? 'Come on, you stupid collection of idiots, pass those books forward, *now*!'

From the back row a volley of at least six books landed heavily on the floor in front of him. They'd each thrown at least one, but he wasn't going to have the whole gang out to perform in front of the rest of the class. Carefully, he picked the boy nearest the gangway.

'Terry.'

'Who, me, sir?' Big, lumbering Terry, with the gaping mouth, slow wits and ready audience for each statement of the obvious.

'Come here and pick up these books.'

Terry walked slowly towards the teacher's desk and then stopped, belatedly aware of a clash of loyalties. He looked back to Barry, as if waiting for instructions. Sensing the importance of the clash, Tony insisted, clearly and firmly, trying to keep the excitement out of his voice:

'Benton, pick up those books and place them on my desk.'

Still no message from Barry. Terry grunted, slowly and deliberately scooped up all the books in his clumsy hands, and Tony breathed an inward sigh of relief.

'Hey, Tes, chuck us one here!' Barry shouted.

A gleam of recognition, and Terry had scattered all the books across the room; most landed open, some with pages torn, and there was one pathetic half-cover still clenched awkwardly in his hand. He grinned nervously at his teacher.

Tony Jenkins felt the frustrations of the entire week well up as he noticed how close they were, swung his right arm and slapped Terry Benton across the face once, very hard.

'Cor!'

'D'you see that?'

Terry stared, disbelieving, trying not to cry. His cheek was red. Barry, confident and threatening, stood up.

'You shouldn't have done that.' Tony ignored him.

'Hey, Jerky, you shouldn't have done that.'

'Sit down, Edwards, or I'll do it to you.'

'You try it. Just you try it, Jerky.'

A challenge, open and deliberate, and there was nothing he could do. He couldn't hit Barry Edwards, and they both knew it. Take him to Archer and admit he'd belted Terry for throwing some books? – suicide. There was nothing to do, nowhere to go, nothing to say.

They were all talking by now, excited, frightened and angry. He heard Alice say sharply, 'He shouldn't have done that', and Jenny, his one remaining ally, sat pale and still. Behind the chatter grew a steady rhythm of chanting, quiet at first, but increasingly insistent, 'We want a riot, we want a riot.' Feet drummed on the floor, unseen hands pounded on the desks, an insatiable beat took over the whole room as thirty voices yelled in unison their hate.

'Shut up! *Shut up!*'

A shout, almost a scream.

For a moment they looked at him, almost pityingly. What was he going to say, what could he say? He looked desperately at the reader, hoping the perfect two-page story might be there, the one that will still an angry class as soon as the book is opened.

'Page 33.'

'What page?'

'We're not reading that.' The slap as one book hit the floor. Then the chattering rose again.

'He shouldn't have done that.'

'He daren't hit Barry.'

'Terry'll have his mum up.'

'Never mind, he's only a student.'

'No, he's not, we've got him all year.'

All year? Dear God, thought Tony, I can't take another week of this. What was it they said – 'Hitting kids may not help them, but by God it makes you feel better.' How wrong could you get? He shouldn't have hit him, it was as clear and simple as that. But he had.

Mercifully, other classes were packing up. The jungle telegraph, the 'feel' of five to four, was clearly being broadcast through the building. In sixty class-rooms, pens were being slid into pencil cases, coats were being slipped on, whispered assignations made and over a thousand minds were already halfway down the drive.

'Wait. You're not going till someone's owned up for bursting that paper bag.' Hoots of derision, and a battery of hostile stares greeted this latest pronouncement. But he had to; couldn't they see – he'd made a threat, he couldn't just ignore it. So this is teaching, he thought, a lad hit, his parents on their way to school, a class riot, and Mr Tony Jenkins concerned for an empty bag of crisps.

'It wasn't me, sir,' said Jenny unnecessarily.

Tony stood by the door, wondering what he was going to do. No one would own up, that was obvious. If he stayed where he was, he could physically stop them getting out, but what mightn't they do if he kept them all in? And then there was Alice, and Andy and Ted . . . or was it Bill? Perhaps it had been Terry? But he couldn't give Terry a detention now, not with his cheek still red and parents probably on the warpath. Who else could it have been?

There was a light tap on the door. He turned to see his mate John wink, wave and pass on, ignoring the chaos and the strain that must be all over Tony's face. That's what friends were for, except that John never seemed to have any trouble with kids, and for the moment that made him an enemy. Then he remembered: John was going early, bang on 4 o'clock. If he wanted a lift home he'd have to let them go. If he kept them that meant the bus, maybe even waiting at the same bus stop. No, there were things you couldn't face, shouldn't be asked to face. He didn't mind humiliation, but he wasn't going home on a bus with Edwards and cronies shouting 'Jerky' after him.

The bell went.

PART ONE: PROBLEMS

Chapter 1

Practical Problems

Only a hermit knows nothing about discipline in schools. The Press and TV, gossip and rumour, memory and anecdote all combine to circulate a spectacular, contradictory selection of evidence about the state of contemporary schools, and the problem is much less to collect information than to organise it into some coherent and intelligible pattern.

This book neither attempts to establish the current extent of indiscipline, nor seeks to compare the present situation with that in the past. Measurement in such an area is notoriously difficult, and invariably biased by prejudices which seek the support of evidence but remain unaffected by it. A school population which comprises children of all abilities up to the age of 16 is unprecedented in our educational history, and I have neither the qualifications nor the space for the detailed study of attitudes, teacher and pupil behaviour, assumptions about authority, and overall social change which should inform a serious historical comparison. My humbler, more immediate concern is with the present, and with the problems which may confront the young teacher in a contemporary school.

Tony Jenkins may not be real, but his problems are. 'Out of Control', clearly, is not offered as a 'typical' lesson, and many teachers will complete their initiation without such drastic crises, but a glimpse of the worst does at least suggest the seriousness of the problem. Statistically it may be indefinable, but in personal terms the losses in such a situation are heavy – for the teacher, the effectiveness of his work, and therefore for his pupils as well.

The basic assumption of this book is that it is better to know about trouble than not to, because caution is a surer path to survival than innocence. I have no wish to depress education students, or to suggest that the whole of teaching is a sordid fight for power, since I enjoy my work and care passionately that teaching should attract the ablest, most imaginative people available. But whatever their quality, new entrants to teaching will need to establish some kind of control over their classes, even if their ultimate aim is to transform the nature or diminish the extent of that very control. Paradoxically, it is those of us who most want to change the future meaning of 'what teaching is' who most need to attend to the problems of the present. Our effectiveness in the class-room, our work with kids and the room for manœuvre left us by authorities and public opinion, will all be determined by our success in confronting the initial questions of discipline, and no normal school offers its teachers any way of side-stepping the complex ethical and practical problems involved in the act of control. In the long term, more satisfying and attractive structures can be created, but it would be a rash probationer who concerned himself solely with the long term.

Newspapers, personal experience and some dramatic case histories all testify that young teachers can face serious difficulties. Most are left to work out their own salvation more or less alone, and the core of this book discusses how that can best happen, but as a starting-point it is necessary to identify the roots of these difficulties, beyond the class-room in which they occur.

The shrillest accounts offer the simplest explanations, and for so complex a phenomenon it is not enough to blame TV, atheism or the end of National Service. Tony Jenkins, for instance, did not come to grief because of a single identifiable error, but because of an inter-action of various factors, many of which might be changed or improved. No one could guarantee to make teaching easy, but it should be possible to disentangle some of the strands involved in the tangle of failure.

Preparation

We begin where the teacher begins, with his training. The traditional view of educational study contrasts it with the work of schools, so that teacher-training institutions (TTIs) are responsible for educational theory, while schools offer the balancing experience of 'teaching practice'. The separation, of course, is not intended to be as absolute as that, but the theory/practice dichotomy reflects the established difference of emphasis between TTIs and schools; in the middle, it is hoped, the student teacher will absorb both forms of experience and incorporate them into his own individual philosophy and work.

Back in the real world, this neat division of labour rarely works smoothly. It conceals an awkward gulf of mistrust between schools and TTIs, whereby mutual suspicion – even contempt – often sabotages any hope of effective co-operation. Also, the 'teaching practice' is often an insulated experience, cut off from a full teaching load and from the deadening knowledge that you have a year to go at least. As a result, many probationers begin their first jobs unprepared for the demands which will be made upon them. In many cases their lecturers will have accustomed them to a style of thinking which is not only unrelated to their new working conditions but actually irreconcilable with them. Immaculately structured lessons, careful preparation, un-limited materials, available resources and positive pupil response are sometimes assumed rather too readily, and the darker side of the picture ignored.

There are good reasons for this. Too heavy an emphasis on likely problems could be unduly depressing, and many education lecturers feel that the problems of control in schools are so various and sub-jective that nothing can usefully be said about them in advance. They therefore concentrate on those areas of the curriculum (educational philosophy and psychology, the teaching of subjects) where there is an accepted wisdom on which to draw and the clear possibility of generalised statement and discussion. Also, some lecturers have more intimate reasons for reticence. Their teaching experience may have been limited to selective schools, or may have begun so long ago that they have seriously forgotten what it feels like to be a struggling teacher. Very few have substantial first-hand experience of compre-hensive schools, and are thus ignorant of their distinctive possibilities, pressures and demands. Others may be all too aware of their former inadequacies as practising teachers and may therefore be naturally eager to bury their past in academic respectability.

Two personal anecdotes illustrate the possible range of response. One formidable and eminent educationalist when asked what he would do if a boy defied him gave an incredulous stare, followed by a massively confident 'he wouldn't't'; impressive, but hardly helpful to his students. At the other extreme, a girl student doing her teaching practice at a school where I taught had a college tutor visit her last lesson in the afternoon when she had a difficult class. After some early trouble-some moments he walked quietly out. By the time the lesson was over he had returned to his college, and she received no comment, criticism or reaction of any kind. With that range of confidence and attitude, it would be silly to expect a uniform approach.

Beneath the variations, however, there is a consistent disdain for matters of discipline which goes deeper than personal taste. The estab-lished tone of academic discussion precludes too sustained an atten-tion to the control of children, since this is felt to belong to a repressive era now safely past. In some areas a valuable emphasis on positive work and creative relationships has hardened into a dogma, so that extreme devotees refuse to countenance the possibility that a child may be lazy, destructive or rude. As a result, many TTI lecturers are sometimes inhibited from exploring adequately with their students one of the most serious threats to their ultimate effectiveness.

The apprehensive student who seeks help on this question may be lucky in finding a sympathetic tutor with relevant experience, but beyond that he will receive no assistance of a structured, organised kind. Few TTIs devote much attention, in the vital forms of teaching time, formal discussion, written assignments or recommended reading, to this area of students' primary concern. Farley's *Secondary Modern Discipline*, for instance, may be a dated and ultimately cynical work, but it is livelier and more directly helpful to students than many of the set educational texts they will be encouraged to read or compelled to buy. Yet how many students hear of Farley, or are given ready access to his book?

The overwhelming experience of young teachers entering non-selective schools is that their training has not prepared them for a large part of the work they have to do. Why it has not, and how it might, are important questions which can only be glimpsed at here (although Chapter 10 offers specific suggestions for the sceptical). But it is not only prejudice which makes embittered teachers allege that their new colleagues frequently join them unprepared and ill-equipped; those same teachers, of course, bear an equal but different responsibility for disciplinary problems. It is important, however, to recognise that at the very outset of the process that will convert him into a teacher, the education student is actively if unwittingly discouraged from thinking about one of the key issues in his future work.

Organisation

Once in the school, of course, the problems multiply, and it is in the school that most of them have to be solved. The struggling probationer may well, like Tony Jenkins, go ruefully back to his training and wonder why they missed *that* out, but in the presence of chaos he needs some more immediate answers.

In Tony Jenkins's case, there were a number of contributing factors. In the first place, his relationship with the school was entirely negative; he had been allocated a room and a class but little else, and the central truth of his day was that he was alone, him with them, or him against them. The books he had were the only ones that were left, his colleagues were either suffering equally and therefore no help, or having no trouble and therefore a painful reproach. Mr Archer, the headmaster, was remote and alien, as much a threat to Tony as to his class, an impersonal figurehead from a world where children do as they are told and appearances are always impeccably preserved.

This is a dramatically distorted picture, in no way intended as 'average'. In that extreme form, though, it does illustrate a real phenomenon – the isolation of teachers in their rooms and the inability or refusal of their colleagues to help them. Again, the roots of this pattern are complex, going into the social history of schools and the prized tradition of teacher independence (set against the power of Church or State, rather than that of pupils), but its effects are felt in most schools, and for most probationers they are damaging.

Our whole system has conventionally been hierarchical. The way we pay our teachers, organise our classes, build our schools and allocate our resources are all related to an orthodox set of priorities: academic takes precedence over practical, able over less able, conformist over rebellious, old over young, and so on. The pyramid and the ladder dominate our thinking, and thus prevent us from questioning more radically the way our schools are organised.

In terms of discipline, this means that far too many schools still work on a sliding-scale of severity, whereby both crime and punishment achieve a certain rating: a trivial offence may be dealt with by a prefect, but if he is defied he will call in a teacher; if a teacher has difficulty he will consult his head of department and refer the guilty child to him, and serious cases will be dealt with by a senior mistress, master or deputy head. Ultimately, with all the finality of capital punishment, the very darkest sins go to 'The Head', the top of the pyramid, whose judgement is final and whose word is law. And then, after the caning, admonishment or suspension, they all go home, and life goes on next day.

The real problem about this ladder is that it requires that each person on it be more effective as a punishing agent than the person lower down. If a probationer teacher has trouble with a rude girl who will make mincemeat of his head of department, the ladder will not work and the system will break down. But discipline is not all-important, and appointments to responsible posts should not be made solely on the capacity of the teacher involved to frighten children, so that it may well be that those on lower rungs of the ladder are better equipped for specifically disciplinary tasks than those above them.

More generally, the expectations of the disciplinary ladder impose great strains on those with power and frustrate those without it. The deputy head who has been appointed 'with responsibility for discipline' will feel himself expected to be continually effective, better than anyone else, at the negative and limited job of controlling kids. Because of that, he may well be drawn into extreme actions or prolonged battles which his judgement tells him are against the best interests of the pupil, the school and himself, but to which his unreal role seems to commit him. He may feel that he cannot be seen to lose, and must therefore sustain pressure or enforce rules in circumstances where it may be unproductive or positively dangerous to do so.

At the bottom of the ladder, meanwhile, teachers less well-paid will assume that their financial inferiority means that they are less responsible for order than their superiors, but they will also complain if those superiors are incapable of carrying out the functions for which they appear to have been elevated. Young teachers who have gone through the ignominy of 'sending that pest Tucker to the Head' may be doubly grieved by the result, not only that Tucker goes away thinking that they cannot cope with him, but also that he comes back very little different. No teacher has the power instantly to change a child's personality, but the ladder sometimes encourages the assumption that he has this power or the expectation that he ought to be able to acquire it.

Within this general framework the belief has become widespread that each individual teacher is responsible for what goes on in his class-room, and that only in times of dire crisis or extreme emergency should other members of staff become involved. Certainly this is the message received by many probationers: 'I felt very inadequate at first, but my head of department did much to encourage me. I felt disinclined to approach him too often, not because he would not help but because I then regarded seeking advice as failing in my job.' Or: '. . . if it is left to the new teachers themselves many of them, despite facing frightening experiences, will be reluctant to seek help, feeling that such action is tantamount to an admission of failure.'

These are two extracts from a small personal collection of friends' reminiscences about their probationary year in teaching, and although that does not make them statistically sound I am nonetheless sure that the view they provide is general. The class-room walls and door, as the orthodoxy goes, are your kingdom and your boundaries, and if kids come out or other teachers go in with any kind of regularity, then something must be wrong.

There are good side-effects from this doctrine, like the freedom allowed to many individual teachers and the consequent variety of approach that many kids encounter, and it is also true that many young teachers feel instinctively that they want to make their first mistakes in private. This is all very well, provided that the results of those mistakes are also private, and do not extend beyond the occasion of the original incident and the people involved in it; more often, however, teaching mistakes contribute to an erosion of order and a cumulative worsening of the working atmosphere, to which some early outside intervention or support might be a corrective. The hierarchical tradition ensures that many young teachers either do not look for such assistance, or feel inadequate and guilty if it is offered. Conversely, many more experienced staff are reluctant to offer help or advice, either for fear of being snubbed or else because their contribution may be seen as a genteel insult, a camouflaged suggestion that the recipient cannot cope.

Finally, the overall hierarchical structure can inhibit the proper development of teachers even after their first difficulties. Once a teacher, particularly a young teacher with energy and imagination, has ensured some kind of initial survival, a platform from which more positive exploration can proceed, he needs the opportunity to extend his limits: to teach in teams, or across departments; to take out trips, initiate activities and launch ventures which may not ultimately succeed. In the hierarchical situation a cautious Head or head of department may well be more aware of the pressure of those above him than the needs of those below, and if he is responsible for all that happens, it is easier to play safe and do things the way he did last year. As a result, risks are not taken, innovations are not sanctioned, and possible opportunities for marrying energy and experience are lost. Defiantly, the would-be innovator goes it alone and achieves a mixture of success and failure; he takes the success as his justification, his superiors take the failure as theirs, and somewhere in the middle the kids are faced with a baffling choice of loyalties and waste of resources.

Collaboration ought to be the norm within schools, over the institution generally, and within houses and departments particularly, but far too often this is not the case. A physical education teacher writes about her first year's experience, and the contribution made to it by her head of department:

'Lessons seemed to go all right although I did lack confidence in the beginning. One particular reason for my difficulty was my head of department. When I had been in the school for three weeks both he and the head of girls' PE came in to watch a gymnastics lesson, my one and only during the week. Afterwards I felt as if I should never have dared to call myself a teacher. Neither of them said a word. Mr Harley then said we should talk about the lesson. I felt really humiliated, but wanted to hear what he had to say, because I knew I could justify my reasons for choosing the material I had used. I never heard anything again. I do not know to this day what he thought.

'My confidence was not boosted by the fact that I was never given any form of responsibility, not even on Sports Day. Other members of my department would be up to their eyes in work and I would be completely free. When I asked if I could help, I was sent out to play like a 3-year-old child. Then I did not ask to help any more. I felt humiliated and inadequate.'

Naturally, this is not a typical experience. Many heads of department do not inhibit their members of staff, and some actively assist them. But the hierarchical structure of the school does encourage a vertical relationship between teachers which frequently becomes divisive, and this not only complicates the task of the struggling young teacher but also fragments the school atmosphere, breaking down any notion of a unified approach. Large comprehensive schools are probably healthy in that they usually defeat any narrow attempt to impose a limiting style of behaviour on all their children, but there is still a sense in which staff need to be united, even if they are not always agreed. Hierarchy defeats this aim, despite the irony that those sitting astride the pyramid are often those who call most stridently for a common line or an agreed set of standards.

Only the active involvement of all members of staff, using to the full their talents, insights and experience, can ensure their full co-operation. More precisely, it is in many cases only possible to achieve a sane working atmosphere and a set of creative teacher-pupil relationships if all staff are heavily involved, so that participation may be a means not only to exploration and experiment, but also to the less dramatic but equally necessary goal of order. The very hierarchical structure which has come to symbolise order and is used so forcibly to achieve it can also be a serious threat to its achievement.

Teachers and Kids

The probationary teacher, however, has more urgent needs than the eventual democratisation of schools. Whatever the quality of his training or the structure of the school at which he starts work, he will by any realistic forecast be compelled to direct the efforts and energies of numerous classes of kids, and it is likely that he will make some mistakes.

The sketchy introductory analysis so far offered is in no way intended to suggest that all probationary teachers are innocent victims of a mindless system, determined to crush their infant talents and reduce them to a tweedy, chalkbound mediocrity. Both TTIs and schools may well make the job more difficult, but a large number of probationary howlers are of the teacher's own making, and it would be amazing if this were not so.

Any education student who can precisely predict the nature of his or her mistakes is rare, since the worst mistakes are by definition those he least expected. In those circumstances, it is therefore worth sampling vicarious disasters, both as a specific warning against particular mistakes and as a more general consolation that everyone else was pretty hopeless too – they just learned to hide it better.

'My main mistake at first was to regard the children as machines or automatons. When I said jump I expected them to, and when they did not I lost confidence. I thought then that it was because I was hopeless in the job. Gradually I learned to approach people in various ways. I was not always consistent enough, and this was mainly because I was not sure what I was aiming for, so the children felt insecure too.'

'When I first started teaching, I was mainly concerned that the children should like me; I wanted to be popular – whatever that is. Looking back, I feel that I must have sacrificed quite a lot to achieve this and I was completely unprepared when with certain groups it began to backfire on me.'

'I tended to lose my temper and show my irritability too often, which the children enjoyed. I learned from that too. Because of this there were a few pupils who always won in any kind of confrontation. These pupils were usually rude and not very bright. I probably expected too much from them and spoke above their level. In spite of making all these mistakes I did enjoy teaching; my lesson failures usually occurred because I had not prepared fully enough or had misjudged the capabilities of the form.'

'When I discussed my discipline problems with people they almost invariably told me I had been "too nice". Had I been rather cold and stern at first and "let them know who's boss", I was assured, I could have thawed and they would still have respected me. I am still not sure what this respect is, or whether I have it even now. Probably not. All I know is that I no longer blame all my problems on the fact that I am short, female, look rather younger than I am and tend to squeak when I raise my voice. After two years life is that bit easier. I am a bit tougher and things are on the whole much more enjoyable.'

In teaching there is no one way to disaster, any more than there is a single route to success, but those who get better do so by watching their own and others' mistakes, and borrowing a whole repertoire of 'things that sometimes work'. Teaching problems cannot ultimately be reduced to an exhaustive outline, since the problems are presented by the kids; in many cases, indeed, the problems are the kids. TTIs, schools and teachers may all do their worst (and sometimes they do), but anyone interested in teaching in general and in discipline in particular must eventually consider the customers:

'Perhaps the most disturbed and disturbing pupil was Chris, who persisted in adding sexual appendages to the pictures in the book we used. I could never prove it was him particularly, as some of the books were already defaced. I dreaded that other teachers who used the same set of books would complain about their state, and spent many hours after school erasing the graffiti; fortunately, Chris rarely had a pen.'

'He was naughty in a strangely sullen way, would declare loudly and at regular intervals "This is crap", and began muttering swear words just loud enough for me to hear but soft enough to be able to deny it if challenged. This sort of thing I thought it best to ignore, but he would also do crazy things, like pulling chairs from under people, teasing and fighting. I felt strangely powerless with this particular boy, as I knew that the majority of the class were looking to me to do something and yet nothing I tried seemed to work. Punishing him had no effect. I often kept him behind after the lesson to talk to him and he always remained completely silent, except on one occasion when he burst into tears, and would never look at me while I talked.'

'One of the most difficult of the boys was a hulking lad called Kevin. Star of the school soccer team, his interest was sparked only by football and ferrets. Faithful to my training I endeavoured to pursue these interests but Kevin remained hostile; on one occasion he arrived in the class with a length of copper wire which he wound round the desk legs in repeated attempts to trip me up.'

'The difficult girls in the group I found really puzzling. They were on the whole brighter than the boys, seemed to enjoy the lessons at first and had produced some pretty good work. But then about five or six of them formed a little knot at the back of the room, and what began as just the odd giggle became progressively more serious as the year went on. Attempts to separate them would take up about five minutes of each lesson, for though I had forbidden them to sit together they would always make straight for the back and cause quite a racket if anyone else had the temerity to sit there. They were often insolent, would refuse to work, forget books and pens, and sometimes make personal comments which would upset me far more than the kind of misbehaviour I got from the boys.'

If that were a true reflection of how all kids behave all the time, I should refuse to be a teacher. It can be that bad, but it can also be much better, and it is with making teaching better that this book is concerned. The starting-point for a study of discipline, all the more necessary because intensely personal considerations can come to override all else, must be that confrontations between teacher and pupil take place within an organisational context which extends far beyond both. TTIS and schools both bear some responsibility for the effects their arrangements have upon a young teacher's subsequent performance, but so too does the climate of ideas in which he operates and to which we all contribute. To achieve effective discipline, and therefore to function clearly, constructive action is required. But there is also an urgent need that some good, hard thinking be done.

Chapter 2

Intellectual Confusion

Discipline is a powerfully emotive subject, because the feelings associated with control are deep and lasting, for both controller and controlled. It takes, therefore, only the briefest selection of disciplinary crises – like those given at the end of the previous chapter, or the selection provided by newspapers in an average month – for passionate controversy to be aroused. People care about discipline, particularly about discipline in schools, and this means that it is both difficult and necessary that we should think about it.

However, thinking is extremely complex, since we have to deal with attitudes towards discipline which are themselves a part of the problem as well as a commentary upon it. A teacher's expectations, a child's view of how a teacher ought to behave, a parent's pattern of punishment, and a community's ideas about the way schools ought to be controlled, are all influences upon the situation that confronts the individual teacher. Just as he has to find practical solutions to his difficulties, so he has to evolve some account of his work which renders it intelligible to himself, even if he finally resorts to the cynical philosophy that teaching has no philosophy. Beyond the simply individual area, too, the whole educational system faces problems over discipline which are intellectual as well as practical.

Imagery and Detail

The young teacher has to be prepared to encounter a wide range of impulse and prejudice, both in others and himself, which may lead in a variety of directions and may frequently conflict. Kids ought to be free, and I like peace and quiet now and again, and I don't know what they are all coming to, and there should not be that much litter, and there would be hell to pay if the local paper got hold of that, and what is the point of worrying about whether he has got a school tie, and I am not taking cheek from anyone, and so on. . . .

The discussion of discipline, in fact, is usually conducted through anecdote and imagery rather than through statistics or rational argument. It is doubtful if anyone could produce any important and relevant statistics which would be widely accepted, and in this intense, human area images speak our feelings more accurately. This is true of teachers, as it is of parents, kids and philosophers:

'You've got to draw the line somewhere.'
'Kids have to be shown who is boss. They want to know their place.'
'Freedom's all very well, but you need a foundation to build on.'
'They want a framework, something to cling on to.'
'I believe in self-expression, but there are limits.'
'You can keep open-ended creativity – give me something with a bit of structure.'

Each of these staff-room snippets insists on solidity – lines are drawn, buildings erected, places and boundaries defined, all with the apparent precision of an architect's plan. Spatial regularity means strength, reliability, lasting value; heaven is made of right angles. And yet, as they stand, they mean nothing. The images suggest firmness and precision but do not supply it, and often the fervour of their assertions implicitly denies the very certainty they claim. The teacher who insists 'You've got to draw the line somewhere' is in fact acknowledging how difficult he finds it to draw a line anywhere. He wants the security that accepted boundaries would give him, but has not the confidence to state where those boundaries should be drawn – otherwise he would have no need to resort to such a generalised statement of faith. If any particular line were obvious he would mention it, and if it were widely accepted he would have no need, so the very fact of his affirmation suggests an inward cry for help. I want the feeling of certainty, it says, but where on earth can I find it?

The same kind of insecurity afflicts large numbers of parents. Naturally worried by their own ill-defined role and the daily demands it makes of them, they are further disturbed by what happens to their children when at school. This is an extract from a letter to a local paper, signed 'Doubtful Parent':

'Discipline is lacking in several ways – for instance, I think school uniforms should be worn by pupils under the age of 15. I was standing outside the school one day and noticed this particularly. It looked as though they were turning out from a football match.

'A certain amount of respect should be shown to the teachers. I do not approve of pupils addressing them by their Christian names.

After all, when the pupils leave school they will be expected to address their superiors differently.'

This raises a number of important points. Firstly, it assumes that discipline is a quantitative thing, to be weighed by the pound and increased at will, rather than being a type of relationship; discipline is lacking, discipline should be increased. Secondly, there is the same pursuit of surface precision, concealing profound uncertainty; exactly what is so distinctive about the age of 15, or Christian names? Thirdly, there is the dubious suggestion that school should be a rehearsal for full-time employment, in which modes of address to teachers are decided by the expectations of superiors at work. Each of these assumptions is highly debatable, but from the confident speed with which they are produced it seems unlikely that 'Doubtful Parent' has questioned any of them.

Most revealing of all is the selection of evidence to back up the general charge of indiscipline – Christian names and uniform. Viewed rationally, the clothes a child wears and the name he calls his teacher are hardly central to the learning situation, and yet for many teachers as well as parents these details have acquired enormous potency. What distinguishes these from other disciplinary issues (like failure to do work, bullying, misuse of equipment) is their newness; uniform and Christian names act as a convenient shorthand for a long and bewildering social change. 'Doubtful Parent' almost certainly went to a school where pupils always wore uniform and always used the teacher's full name; the opportunity to do otherwise probably felt quite unreal. Over the last twenty years much else in schools has changed, including the content, teaching method, purpose and meaning of 'work' in school, but it is still the details which capture that change most vividly, so the complaints and questions about apparent trivia in fact express a serious unease about an important and complex transformation.

In that context of suspicion and fear, nothing is trivial. A kid calling me 'Paul' will outrage a conservative observer who fears for the erosion of respect, while revolutionaries will seize on 'sir' as a sign of my imperialist repression of captive pupils. In that last sentence, too, the gap between 'kid' and 'pupils' indicates the extent and delicacy of the problem. 'Kid' is slang and 'pupil' pompous, but 'children' is condescending, 'scholar' prematurely academic, and 'student' ambiguous. But we have to call them something, and in this fiercely personal area we cannot evolve a value-free code like the language of the astronauts. Words and images necessarily involve risk, the chance of saying more or less than we mean, but that is the price we pay for the effort of trying to think more clearly.

The professionals, frequently, are just as vulnerable. Dr Loewenstein,[1] in his report of his research into indiscipline for the NAS, provides an unwitting example of lazy thinking. His title, *Violence in Schools*, indicates the extent to which he is prepared to allow other considerations to tempt him from neutral fact-finding, and both the limited size of his sample and the vagueness of his questions mean, in effect, that nothing of statistical value emerges. One of his findings, for example, is that there were 205 instances of 'aggressive mode of speech or behaviour, refusal to co-operate, disobedience, truancy, etc. and bullying'. Does this really amount to objective, empirical research? Also interesting are his conclusions, where the shadow of prejudice lurks beneath the scholarly impersonality of his prose. He suggests, for instance, that to cure unrest in schools we should: '. . . increase the structure of the curriculum for certain segments of the school population and leave the questioning of values and principles to those more capable of digesting diverse views and concepts.'

Structure again, that solid reassuring cipher with the solid feel – but it is no more than that. For beneath this streaming by orthodoxy (no prizes offered for identifying the 'certain segments of the school population' who should not be encouraged to ask questions) is a blind, traditional faith in the time-table, that symbol of regularity whose geometrical neatness guarantees substance, security and weight. And yet, simply from its grid-like appearance on paper, five squares by eight with a gap for breaks, there is no more reason why the conventional time-table should be a framework or a structure than a cage.

This is how it looks to Richard, a slow, quiet little boy of 14:

'I think school is boring because the lessons are too long and the lessons that are not boring are too short. Some of the teachers make it boring with talking too much. One person I do not like is Mr Jones because he is always nagging on at people and trying to frighten people, but he does not frighten me. There are not many good things about school. The best part at school that I like is the sound of the 4 o'clock bell.'

Not much 'structure' here, and the treatment he is getting fits the traditional pattern perfectly – eight lessons a day, five days a week, of good solid 'subjects'. Real structure, in Richard's terms, might well mean the comfort of being taught much of the time by a teacher he

[1] Loewenstein, *Violence in Schools* (NAS), pp. 29–30.

gets on with, or the knowledge that once every week he would have a whole morning to do something he liked. Something 'structured' in the eyes of the teacher may well be shapeless, purposeless and boring in the eyes of his customers, as numerous immaculately planned courses annually testify. We must keep coming back, and rightly, to look at the actual kids.

Right and Left

It is this failure to look at kids realistically which underlies much of the intellectual confusion in our treatment of discipline. Teachers and parents tend to build vast generalisations on the basis of a very small number of kids they happen to know well, and those without this intimate knowledge resort to distant caricatures, constructed to advance a predetermined thesis rather than to represent the varied, changing human reality of our current school population.

Jean Rowan, for instance, in *The Writing on the Blackboard*, offers a full-length polemic on the state of Britain's class-rooms, with most of her anger directed towards comprehensivisation and a rather sweeping notion of 'modern methods'. She draws on her experiences as a supply teacher (referring to herself as Kate, in a clumsy fictional device) to illustrate her general thesis that our schools are on the verge of a breakdown which is both imminent and widespread. Yet for all her urgency, and her horrified reaction to comprehensive chaos and juvenile depravity (pregnancy is listed as one of the five key discipline problems), she fails to convince any reader who does not already share her prejudices. One extract, her account of a conversation with another teacher about an unruly girl, suggests why:

' "They are untamed", the teacher sighed, after the culprit had been dealt with, "and resistant to all authority."

' "Whatever sort of citizens are they going to make?" Kate asked sadly. "They could reduce us to anarchy. And then, as Plato said, 'once degeneration has set in, democracy is always followed by tyranny'. Can freedom survive?"

' "Probably not", the other teacher replied, with the calm faith of one who sees the human struggle in perspective (she was a devout Roman Catholic). "Half the world is in chains already, and if we go on the way we are going the rest may follow soon." '

The strain of the writing reflects the effort involved. This is an eternal warfare, between absolute good and evil, on a timeless battlefield to which Plato and Roman Catholics have privileged access. Our civilisation is threatened, first with anarchy and then with dictatorship – and all this because a girl ran away to join her friends while Kate was trying to give her a black mark.

What we do not get, here or anywhere else in the book, is a clear, detailed view of the life of the children involved; nor even, despite its autobiographical nature, does Mrs Rowan place us convincingly in the teacher's position, since as a supply teacher she is continually moving from class to class, school to school, strange child to strange child, and her polemical intentions slant every piece of evidence in the book towards her general assertion of crisis. The final acid test, as of any offering in this field, is 'so what?'; given the analysis, however brief or distorted, what action should follow? In Mrs Rowan's case, the argument leads nowhere but to a shaky faith in a possible 13 + examination and a deep but unspecific hunger for the certainties of a mythical past.

In this, she is typical of many reactionaries, who see their traditional values being threatened by such developments as comprehensive schools, community education and unstreamed classes. Her tactical approach, however, of building vast conclusions on small premises, is by no means a monopoly of the educational Right.

At the opposite end of the political spectrum, there are revolutionary theorists who also pay more attention to ideological warfare than to the actual kids in the class-room. In their version of events, discipline is simply a remnant, a relic of teacher oppression, which should be left behind with the authoritarian past from which it came. It can thus safely be ignored by any democratic teacher who believes in the liberation of his pupils.

Some such basic outline underlies the attempts of many young teachers radically to alter the nature of the teacher-pupil relationship. But whatever the objective need for change, much of the thinking through which they argue this transformation is so woolly as to render their efforts not only ineffective but disastrous.

In an article in *Libertarian Education*, b.r.j. (a teacher with some experience) describes his attempts to liberate a class in a Leicestershire high school. His title is 'Discipline Problems', although on both the other occasions when that phrase appears in the text it is placed in inverted commas, as though the problems did not really exist, but were simply dreamt up by the autocrats who are – according to revolutionary theory – ultimately to blame.

For b.r.j., however, discipline problems are real enough. He holds a class discussion, but the kids refuse to listen to each other; he tells them about a book they are to read but gives up because they will not pay attention, and later two pupils who do not like his lessons walk calmly out of the door. The situation would be out of control, except that no attempt to control it has been made. When they will not listen, b.r.j. picks up a paper to read, and when they shout him down he goes home.

This sounds like simple incompetence or psychological weakness, but b.r.j. relates it to a deeper ideological struggle. There are, in his world view, two choices: 'An authoritarian teacher can easily get silence, and never has "discipline problems". A teacher who refuses to impose discipline, naturally creates problems for himself and his students.'[1] Naturally, and if b.r.j. really has been teaching for ten years then he ought to know better. Teachers do not fall neatly into those two categories, and even if they did then the 'teacher who refused to impose discipline' ought to think a lot harder about the problems he thereby creates for his students. b.r.j., however, is far more concerned with his own dramatic act of rebellion ('A teacher who refuses . . . problems for himself . . .') than with the kids it affects. On the evidence of his own account, the kids are frustrated, resentful and bored, but this does not lead him to guilt, anxiety or serious analysis. Instead, he blames the system, and the failure of the LEA to live up to its liberal image:

'But this is Leicestershire, and the official line at the school is liberal, with its talk of "self-discipline" and "self-realisation". How can students learn self-discipline if I constantly impose it? It would seem that I am toeing the official line. But, in that case, why am I having problems? A hostile critic might reply that I am a "bad teacher" – to which my retort would be that I am trying to put into practice what, theoretically, is widespread Leicestershire practice and so should, presumably, cause no problems whatever.'[2]

How naïve can you get? To equate 'self-discipline' for pupils with impotence for teachers is silly and self-defeating, since the chaos which results is patently undisciplined, and clearly fails to serve the selves concerned. Self-discipline may not be the confidence-trick urged by some headmasters, but neither is it a simple matter of teacher abdication. If an authority has an enlightened reputation, that is not to say that every child within that county's boundaries is continually polite,

---

[1] *Libertarian Education*, No. 11, p. 16.
[2] Ibid., loc. cit.

creative and self-sufficient, and thus beyond the need for teachers. Anyone who has seen well-meaning but ill-prepared prophets of revolution in class-room action knows the brief excitement and lasting damage they can cause.

Intellectually, too, this is a recipe for disaster. If there really are only two choices ('An authoritarian teacher . . . a teacher who refuses to impose discipline') then we have all had it, condemned to an eternal toss-up between anarchy and dictatorship. In my experience at least, the truth is a lot more complex and dynamic than that, and therefore more hopeful.

Paradoxically, b.r.j.'s sketch of freedom for the kids comes to nothing because he does not really know who and where the kids actually are; they have become ciphers, part of a plan designed for their benefit but without their being consulted, and the cost paid for this undemocratic revolution is personally high. As one of his pupils says, with innocent, but searing precision: 'It is all so one-sided – all how *you* do things – how *you* want things – what about us?'

More intelligent rebels, of course, do pay proper attention to the kids they teach and as a result produce situations more creative than this and writing far more valuable and stimulating. Many young teachers, understandably, are drawn to the warmth and good sense of Herbert Kohl and John Holt, whose works are made doubly attractive by the frequently turgid quality of their bedfellows in education reading-lists.

So far as reading is concerned, such sources are entirely helpful. In the process of teaching, however, and the transfer of good ideas from paper to action, the assistance must be less direct. You cannot simply decide to teach like Holt and Kohl unless you have their experiences and talents behind you, and in both cases the emotional maturity of the men and their experience of more conventional teaching were quite as important to their success as the ideas and values they sought to promote. Young teachers must necessarily follow their own inclinations and work through their own mistakes, but they would be silly to imagine that they could instantly replicate a success that has taken gifted men a number of years to achieve.

The same applies to English folk heroes like Neill and Michael Duane, both of whom have a dangerously enthusiastic following in teacher-training institutions. Enthusiastic, because their work points in important and unusual directions, dangerous because their situation was different from that encountered by the young teacher who applauds them. Neill operated in a limited world of his own construction, teaching children whose parents had already endorsed his approach; Duane

D

was an impressive headmaster who seems to have established a humane school in a difficult area. Both, however, were experienced teachers using their accumulated wisdom and power as headmasters to establish a specific type of school community.

The average left-wing radical in a comprehensive school is much lower on the ladder of influence, and has fewer resources at his disposal. He also has challenges to face which are more pressing and less grandiose than the restructuring of a whole school; the only kingdom he can claim is the limited and temporary one of the kids he has to teach, and those same kids are shared with a large number of other teachers whose approach and assumptions will probably be quite different. As a result, he will be lucky if he can create the conditions he wants even for brief spells, let alone on any lasting basis. Neill describes the outcome of his own early attempt at a libertarian UDI:

'I had just come under the influence of Homer Lane and was enthusiastic about self-government. In staff meetings I pleaded for it, and finally dear old John Russell said "Good, Neill can have self-government in his classes." Being a young fool I agreed. The sequel of course was that one class came from – say – a maths class with discipline to my geography class . . . and played merry hell, naturally. Teachers in near rooms protested and the experiment failed, and so did I; I left, or was I thrown out? I am not quite sure.'[1]

That is the start of an answer to the question 'How can Summerhill principles be applied to a state school?', and Neill's conclusion is far from encouraging:

'It is sad to say it, but there can be no real freedom in a state school if the Head is not on your side. Hundreds of young teachers would be delighted to have more freedom in their classes but they cannot get it and some tend to become cynical and resigned to their fate. There can be no freedom so long as the Establishment rules that there must not be.'[2]

This need not be the last word (it is, after all, some time since Neill attempted to work within state education) but it does indicate the problems. Teachers can make their classes genuinely democratic communities, but only with talent and a lot of hard work; personally,

[1] A. S. Neill, *Talking about Summerhill* (Gollancz, 1967), pp. 100–1.
[2] Ibid., p. 101.

I have only seen it happen where there was an initial insistence on order and a careful development, staged over at least a year. This spells caution to any revolutionary eager to establish the millennium by Christmas, and it also indicates the intellectual complexity of the teacher's power situation, a complexity we simplify at our peril.

A powerful allegiance (whether to a vision of permissive decay or to a programme of revolutionary change) is a simplifying pressure, and for that reason needs watching. This is not the extremist 'moderate' argument which condemns all extremism with the dogmatic assertion that all truth is compromise and all wisdom 'somewhere in the middle'; complacency and intellectual cowardice are quite as dangerous as commitment or fanaticism. But the pressure, in communications media and elsewhere, is towards the polarisation of argument: democracy or anarchy, flexibility or standards? Is there a crisis? To cane or not to cane? Autocracy or freedom? The strident tone of the questions implies that they have to be answered in their own terms, but this is not the case. The answer to 'A or B?' may in fact, after all, be 'C'.

Philosophy and Discussion

One purpose of this chapter is to demonstrate the extent to which the young teacher today has to do his own thinking. The words of others may be stimulating or useful, but they will need to be continually tested against his own beliefs and experience, because no existing account or prescription will be adequate; indeed, it is partly this sense of unique exploration which makes much teaching exciting as well as difficult, and if all our thinking had been done before we started there really would be cause for alarm.

There is, however, a middle ground between total prescription and total improvisation, and it is in this no man's land that educationalists operate. Few of them presume to offer detailed instructions on how to do the job, but behind the vast output of the 'education industry' must lie the general assumption that reading about education helps students to become better teachers.

Unfortunately, there is little evidence to support this faith in the field of discipline. Those few books which do exist are either discreetly buried, or else bury themselves in a determined effort to translate practical sense into the academically acceptable currency of sociological terms.

There are strong institutional reasons (and often personal professional ones) why a TTI lecturer should not spend too much time or energy discussing the control of children, and the sacred four gospels of Education (History, Philosophy, Psychology and Sociology) ensure that little is done. Rationally, each of the four has a useful potential contribution to make, but few of their exponents have shown much eagerness to oblige. The history of education is concerned more with the names of innovators and the analysis of structural changes than with the study of conditions in past schools; the psychology of education is concerned more with how one child learns than with how a group of children behaves; and the sociology of education is concerned more with categories and generalisation than with the study of social attitudes or the patterns of family behaviour.

Research activity, too, is intrinsically hostile to the study of discipline. The preoccupation with ideal models, fixed situations which can be exactly replicated in other situations, means that most of the flow of human interchange must be lost to the researcher's view. He abhors a variable – but the class-room teems with them and a disciplinary crisis contains little else. Time and money, consequently, are spent on areas more susceptible of control.

We thus have large numbers of capable, experienced teachers, specifically withdrawn from the teaching of children in order to train further teachers or to carry out more specialised types of thinking for us, who have nothing to offer on one of the most difficult areas of teaching concern. Certainly, if teacher-training were to practise its pupil-centred creed and base its own programme on the needs of its students, a lot more time and thinking might be devoted to the practical and intellectual problems which teachers daily confront. As it is, a few euphemisms, some cheery words of reassurance, a couple of hair-raising anecdotes and the rest is silence.

The one area of academic study which might be expected to shed real light is the Philosophy of Education. Even taking into account the philosophers' modest redefinition of their role (from dealers in means, ends and eternal verities to linguistic surgeons), it is reasonable to suppose that this quarter of the educational canon should have something to say.

Professor R. S. Peters, in fact, does deal in some detail with the concept of Authority in *Ethics and Education*, and his treatment makes an interesting illustration of conventional wisdom at work.

To begin with, by writing for both philosophers and educationalists he is taking a large risk and performing a useful bridging function. Also, by writing simultaneously for professionals and students he commits himself to pragmatic, relevant detail, linking theory with practice, the concepts of education with the actual life of schools:

'Schools are institutions whose overriding aim should be that of education which . . . involves the initiation of the young into a worthwhile form of life. This involves activities and forms of thought and awareness which are regarded as intrinsically valuable; involves modes of conduct that are morally justifiable, together with their political derivatives, i.e. behaviour associated with "good citizenship"; it involves manners, decency in dress and speech, cleanliness, etc., which are part and parcel of an approved form of life.'[1]

This is where the problems begin. From unobjectionable, almost trite premises, Peters moves to a highly controversial conclusion about 'decency in dress and speech'. Exactly which standards of decency are the 'political derivatives' of morally justifiable modes of conduct? In dress, for instance, what is meant by decent? Suits? School uniform? Ties? Jackets? Trousers? Skirts? Bikinis? Just who is it that 'approves' the 'approved form of life' to which such features are essential?

It is difficult to resist the conclusion that Peters here has relaxed, allowing a natural, unargued conservatism to penetrate the argument, while the appearance of logical sequence persists. 'Things are like that', he seems to be saying, but from a philosopher we expect more rigour.

To be fair, he is more realistic than many of his colleagues about the conditions in which some teachers have to work. He recognises the existence of difficult schools:

'The conditions of schooling and the attitudes of the inmates make talk of education almost as out of place as a fashion parade on a dunghill. Teaching in such "blackboard jungle" types of institution requires special gifts and probably special training. It is more like a commando operation than an educational exercise, for the problem is basically that of establishing conditions for normal education to take place.'[2]

In one sense this is a helpful, sympathetic admission, and Peters is honest about the philosopher's inability to say much to such a situation; the equation of 'talk of education' with a fashion parade is quite as revealing, incidentally, as that of rough schools with a dunghill. But in the course of this humble disclaimer Peters evades a crucial issue. The selective definition of 'normal' education implies that pupil hostility and inadequate teaching conditions are extreme phenomena,

[1] R. S. Peters, *Ethics and Education* (Allen & Unwin, 1966), p. 252.
[2] Ibid., pp. 279–80.

rarely encountered by teachers. They are thus disturbing but different, and unconnected with the genuinely *educational* concern that is the philosopher's rightful province. Yet in many schools, in the hinterland between Manchester Grammar and the blackboard jungle, there are hordes of teachers not in perpetual strife, but worried by their power struggles with kids, and sorely in need of a way to understand such situations as well as to control them. This is an urgent ethical problem, and it is disappointing to find it so rapidly evaded.

Professor Peters, meanwhile, addresses himself to the concept of Authority, which might seem to be a promising start. Such a discussion is in fact the closest approach educational philosophy makes to discipline problems in school, but the conditions of intellectual entry are severe: '. . . there must be some acceptance of the value of the task on the part of the pupils. Without this commands mark the point at which authority begins to degenerate into power.'[1]

'There must' has logical, but not practical force. Peters here defines the territory with which he is concerned, and one of its features is the acceptance by pupils of the value of whatever they are doing. That is an integral part of the notion of Authority, and once that prerequisite is absent we have moved into the murkier world of Power.

That movement, however, between accepted Authority and asserted Power, is one that teachers constantly have to make; at the very point of Peters's borderline, between acceptance and rejection, agreement and argument, our most crucial decisions have daily to be made. Peters's use of 'degenerate', unfortunately, makes it crystal clear that this continual traffic is vertical as well as horizontal, not only between different territories but also between various levels of an intellectual hierarchy.

Up there is Authority, cool, rational and worthy of study; down here is Power, hectic, busy and resistant to conceptual analysis. If Authority, however, presupposes widespread acceptance, it presents few problems – primarily those concerned with the uses to which such influence is put, and the definition of abuse. Where the work and the thinking become difficult is in the territory of Power, where there is no acceptance, but only assertion, conflict and bluff. In that area it is much harder to make clear distinctions or confident pronouncements, and for that reason the conventionally valued resources of educational philosophy are invariably directed elsewhere, to an insulated ideal model of 'education'. What happens in schools, apparently, is a different matter.

[1] Ibid., p. 267.

All that can confidently be salvaged from this brief survey of think-ing about discipline is the gloomy thought that teachers, parents, extremists and philosophers are just as liable to prejudice, abstraction, lazy thinking and mental cowardice as the rest of us. Ultimately, how-ever, that is a positive conclusion, since it underpins the obvious truth that we have to think for ourselves. In this area of education more than any other, there can be no remote expert to whom we turn; you can have an authority on Authority, but only a fool pontificates about control. This leaves the responsibility placed securely on those with whom it belongs, the teachers, parents and pupils involved. It is for them to resolve their own intellectual confusion, through a sharing of insights in which each carefully tests words and images against the reality he knows. In this gradual and communal process, probationary teachers can and should take part, but the gains of such a discussion will far transcend the immediate limits of class-room struggles for power. For only through an intelligent and flexible discussion do we become aware of the reality of other lives, become capable of breaking down the caricatures and slogans into actual people, genuine feelings and real situations, and so gain the maturity and objectivity to teach well.

PART TWO: CLOSE-UP

Chapter 3

Actual Kids

Stereotypes

We begin, necessarily, with kids. Kids are kind and cruel, stupid and responsive, direct and devious, emotional and insensitive—in fact they ultimately possess all the virtues and vices of their parents and teachers. In the business of talking about them it is clearly convenient to try and simplify the endless variations, to reduce the complex mass to a single imaginary child, and to pretend that we deal only with him – multiplied thousands of times. Such a simplifying process is natural, occasionally necessary and always dangerous. For the stereotype has only to last for a couple of paragraphs and it becomes the virtual subject; methods and approaches in the author's mind are tailored to suit the stereotype, and the stereotype is adjusted to match existing conditions, established practice or the prejudices of its creator. Proposals already decided on are checked against the revised reality of an imaginary figure, and come to seem increasingly 'realistic'. So, as we debate what to do with the 'high fliers', 'ROSLA kids' or 'the slow learner', Ian, Jenny and Colin slip quietly out of sight.

A whole tradition of educational inquiry has sanctified this process, from the Taunton Commission onwards. Its culmination was the Norwood Report's confident classification of children into Academic, Technical and Practical which resulted, not quite by accident, in the tripartite system of secondary schools introduced after the 1944 Education Act. Stereotypes immortalised in brick.

It is not only the élitists, however, who fall prey to the charms of caricature. The most powerful stereotype in currency at the moment, and the one most relevant to the discussion of discipline, has far less traditional charm. What I call the Disadvantaged Victim is conveniently exemplified by Billy Casper in Barry Hines's novel *Kestrel for a Knave*, and its equally excellent film version *Kes*. As a character, Billy is a forceful, convincing creation who directs our attention to an area of artistic as well as educational neglect. As a caricature, however, simplified by the enthusiasm of his intellectual fans, Billy Casper can be a powerfully emotive distraction. The scruffy, aimless kid from a broken home is real enough, and so are his problems in school, but a number of factors in the presentation slant both book and film in Billy's favour. In the first place, he is an individual set against an imperfect system, and he thus evokes in sympathetic watchers and readers common feelings of exclusion, uncertainty and loss.

More precisely, Billy is presented as a passive victim – the small, helpless prey of a vicious world, a competitive society and an insensitive school. He loses his fights, his elder brother knocks him about, he defends himself but does not attack others – all of which makes him more attractive but need not be a consequence of his deprivation; many actual deprived children steal, destroy property and attack innocent victims. One boy I taught, who came from a similar background, threatened to beat up his younger brother if he got a good report; that too might be a response to a hostile world, but it also smells of terrorism. Billy Casper, by contrast, is guilty only of venial sins; his stealing is petty, his obscenity witty or defiant, and his rebellion either hilarious or moving.

He is presented from within, so that he appears unlucky rather than destructive or stupid. If, for instance, he was incapable of reading the book on falconry or of holding the class spellbound with his account of training Kes, he might not have gained so many intellectual fans. More cynically, it is difficult to imagine a similarly successful work which was centred on a fat, ugly girl of 14 with no friends, interests or enthusiasm, who does not want to do anything but pick her nose, scribble on a desk and listen to pop records.

So far as teaching is concerned, the compassionate bias in the characterisation of Billy Casper glosses over the problems such children present to a teacher. The boy I have taught who was most like Billy also had a great interest in falcons and was a failure in most school subjects. He earned a place in the school Rugby team, but rarely attended practices. In school he spent a lot of time threatening younger boys, shouting insults in the playground, carving on desks and bullying a highly disturbed boy in his form. I seldom heard him speak sensibly, even in answer to calm and reasonable questions, as he preferred to mutter or whisper to his friends and confined his public utterance to a succession of animal noises carefully and accurately aimed at infuriating his teachers. On the one occasion when I managed to find a book on falcons he flicked through the pictures for five minutes and then gave up. I imagine his home background was similar to Billy's, and certainly he provided as great a challenge to the educational system.

I stress the unattractive side of his nature because that was what most of his teachers saw most of the time. Certainly there were staff who knew him more deeply and taught him much better than I did, but all the characteristics which I have mentioned would remain part of their picture of him. This catalogue of vices does not mean that he was less worthy of attention than his more accessible contemporaries, but it does underline the difficulties facing any teacher who seriously intends to be of any use to such a kid. Too easy an adulation of one figure, or too impulsive an emotional response, may blind us to the intricate problems of dealing with actual kids, and imply that we have only to cater for the stereotype for all to be well. Sympathy is not enough.

Any caricature or stereotype must leave out 90 per cent of the kids under discussion. As one powerful image dominates the argument, so other opposing images are defined and propagated, but each one needs to be carefully and regularly tested against the reality of all the kids in a school. Such a reappraisal, too, can penetrate the ideological haze and so illuminate the genuinely comprehensive nature of our task. Just as staff meetings often concern themselves with the top 5 per cent ('Will X get an Oxbridge place this year?') and the bottom 5 per cent ('Y has really gone too far this time – something has got to be done'), so wider educational debate sometimes implies that we only really care about pupils whose ultimate destination will be university or gaol. However, although there are some we like, some we get through to in time and some we will never be able to handle, we do have to teach them all.

Six Portraits

The true corrective to stereotypes is not a fresh range of stereotypes, but varied, individual particularity. I now offer brief portraits of six pupils whom I taught in one academic year. They are deliberately varied in age, temperament and attitude, and all six presented me with distinct challenges and opportunities, both as an authority figure and as a teacher. None of them was outstanding in an academic or criminal sense, but each one had to be thought about – like any other kid.

GERRY Gerry was tall, long-haired and casual. By the time I met him he was doing 'A' level, one of the few intellectuals in a small sixth form. In many ways he was the ideal product of a new comprehensive, an 11+ failure raised to the threshold of higher education. Only Gerry did not fancy it; at the beginning of the year he had thought that he would teach, but by the end of it he had seen enough of teachers and was certain he was going to have a look at other worlds before coming back to this one. Scruffy in appearance and idle in manner, his essays appeared rarely and behind time. In discussion he was lively and original, tenacious in defending his own ideas and impatient with platitudes.

Earlier in his school career he had apparently been less articulate and far more rebellious, but had shrewdly acquired the knack of manipulating appearances. This is part of an essay he wrote for me describing his life in the fourth year:

'School life became unbearable, the pupils rebelled against Authority. Authority acknowledged our rebellion, and we were forced to walk in single file and not talk, in or out of school in between lessons. House facilities were denied, and silence was enforced in the dinner hall. I had a fantastic grudge against Authority and showed it in lessons and my attitude to work; consequently, I was told that unless my attitude changed, I would not be accepted for a fifth year. A teacher told me how to cope with the situation; I took his advice, which was to pretend interest in every subject, and to sound sincere when apologising. It worked, and teachers praised me immensely at the following parents' evening.'

In the light of such experience, Gerry was unimpressed with the shallow seniority accorded to the handful of sec. mod. pupils who had stayed on into the sixth form, since they were granted the privilege of performing supervision duties otherwise carried out by staff. He was critical of much in the school, and resented the appearance of democracy being grafted onto a school council which had no real power. Although he hoped to have a couple of 'A' level passes by the time he left, it would not have broken his heart to have had none, and when he left he had made no application for further education or for jobs.

MARION Marion was neat, quiet and very shy. Boringly well-behaved, she would smile interminably but say very little above a whisper. Both her work and her appearance were meticulously arranged, but neither carried much sign of individual flair. When I first taught her she would hardly say anything, and despite being good at poetry she deeply resented being asked to write poems. She revealed little of her feelings, hopes or ambitions, but was invariably pleasant and polite.

When persuaded to discuss it, she said she felt that the school's discipline was too slack, and she complained that she and her fellow-prefects were constantly being cheeked by junior pupils. She regretted the absence of an overall sense of order, and argued that teachers were too remote to know how bad the situation was. Of the many schools she had been to, she liked best a small secondary modern school where she had known all the teachers. She was not miserable with us but was nonetheless keen to leave after her CSEs, simply because as an RAF child she had become accustomed to a pattern of moving regularly and was restless after three years in the same place.

TERRY   Terry came into the fourth year barely literate, with a string of reports behind him, all of which must have read E for attainment, A for effort. He found the act of writing physically difficult, and although he wished to stay on for an exam course no one was really surprised that his eventual CSE was ungraded. He was not gifted in English, and spoke with little more fluency than he wrote, but he was nonetheless determined to grapple with whatever ideas or material were fed his way.

In lessons, his attitude and behaviour were always excellent. He worked hard to try and understand difficult passages, was prepared to ask questions with an openness which few kids would have dared to risk, and he slogged for hours over essays which took his peers less than half the time. Around the school he was helpful and friendly, and his application brought him some success in craftwork and after he left, national recognition in sport. He left with very little in the way of paper, but he was a joy to teach.

SUSAN   Susan arrived in the middle of the third year, a rangy, athletic girl with a toothy smile and long hair, and by the end of her first term she had established herself as an outstanding pupil. Having been gifted at languages in her previous school, she took to a third foreign language with no hesitation and her parents' discreet hopes for a university career did not seem at all unrealistic. She made close friends with another girl very quickly, was talented at sport and in singing, and around the school, was lively, cheerful and co-operative.

Then, dramatically, she changed. She split up with her friend, suffered a nasty period of unpopularity with other girls during which she was often lonely and depressed, and emerged eventually as a member of an often wild gang of girls, who had once previously attacked her. She hacked her hair into a harsh skinhead cut, and became increasingly rude towards teachers, uninterested in her work and disruptive in lessons, although she retained at times a painfully acute sense of the change that had taken place:

'I like to have a bit of fun, but sometimes I go too far and end up in trouble. I lose my temper too quick with teachers, and end up swearing at them and again get into trouble. I am just a bloody troublemaker wherever I go. I have a foul mouth and cannot control my language. My mum always tells me about this, but it's just a habit. I am quite nervous and cannot leave my nails alone. If my nails are gone I even start on my toe-nails but that gets too tiring (believe it or not, it's true). . . .

'I can tell you I have put up with lots of upsetting things and I think I have had a lot of patience with everybody, the things they have said, that they have even done to me. I put up with people teasing me and I can assure you everybody does it. I don't know what is the matter with me at times, everybody is against me and there is nothing I can do really just fight back and lose.

'I like people to know me and know how I feel about things, not treat me as though I were a kid. I like my life and I don't, if you get what I mean.'

PETE Pete had a lively, chirpy face which was invariably covered by the mat of straight dark hair which flopped about his head. Nothing he did seemed considered or controlled: his uniform, scrupulously provided and cared for at home, seemed to disintegrate into decay the minute he entered school, and his books were invariably dog-eared and ink-stained.

At his junior school, Pete had been the star pupil – quick, intelligent and lively in drama and discussion. In the larger size and wider spread of the comprehensive, however, his apparent supremacy of attainment was no more than average, and he was clearly disappointed to have lost the eminence and approval that his earlier success had brought him.

Even in the third year he was still intolerably talkative. He frequently interrupted with his own immediate concerns, rather than with anything of relevance to other people or to the topic under discussion. His confidence in drama eventually narrowed into a dreary concern with initiating fights as soon as possible. With written work he was impatient to finish, reluctant to explore anything in detail and obsessed with satisfying a minimum quota rather than with producing anything worthwhile. He had often 'forgotten' his book, and was quite happy to respond loudly to any form of distraction which the lesson might provide.

VICKY Vicky's glasses, wispy hair and soft, deliberate voice gave her a quaint, grandmotherly air, and her Tyneside accent and cautious smile made her a distinctive if unobtrusive character. She was shy, but completely helpful and quite willing to talk within a small group, once she had got to know the people involved. She had a quiet serenity that surrounded her through a variety of potentially nasty or boring situations, and I cannot remember ever having seen her bad-tempered or mean. Her work was conscientious, and her behaviour in lessons never earned anything but praise. There was only one snag: she was present in school for an average of three days a week. Sometimes the absences were staggered, sometimes regular; occasionally she would come for a long stretch, and then be away for a similar period. The absence notes came regularly, and gave a variety of excuses, but over each academic year throughout her school attendance Vicky missed 40 per cent of her lessons.

These six kids were not especially hard cases. Those teachers who pride themselves on the intransigence of their pupils could easily produce a more threatening array. But the point of this collection is not the awe they instil, but the variety of personality and background which they share between them, and therefore of skills and insights demanded of their teachers. All over the country, kids like this are taught in batches of thirty, but even six of them amply demonstrate the complexities implicit in that process.

At first sight, these examples have little to do with discipline, since only Susan caused any real trouble, and even she started off as an ideal pupil. But Gerry had been a discipline problem, Terry could easily have been, Pete was with some teachers, and Vicky might have done better in terms of attention if she had followed suit. The urgency with which we think about kids is often sadly proportionate to the likelihood of their disrupting our lessons, and it is sometimes worth asking why children behave well, as well as why they do not. Marion, for instance, was never any trouble to anyone, and for that reason her views were widely ignored. She was a reactionary, but neither clever enough to excite the academics nor lively enough to stir the revolutionaries. She carried on in her own world quite happily, completing all the work she was set, doing as she was told and vainly trying to get junior pupils to do what she had been told to tell them to do. Very little notice was taken of her achievements or her complaints.

The purpose, then, of presenting these miniatures, is to demonstrate the range of needs a teacher in a comprehensive school may try to satisfy. These needs are not only different but in some cases contradictory, and you will not encounter the kids in the orderly one-at-a-time pattern of my descriptions. Marion, as I have explained, was easy to ignore, but to answer her disciplinary demands fully would mean severely punishing Susan every time she had a tantrum and harassing Vicky every time she was absent, neither of which would assist the pupils concerned. Compromise is inevitable, and must be decided by the teacher's inclinations and talents as well as by the needs of the kids.

Among any group of pupils, attitudes will obviously vary, but so too will the factors significant to an understanding of behaviour – in one case, for instance, home background may be decisive, whereas in another peer group relationships within school may be more important. More complex still, the same factor may well have a different significance for each individual. The school hierarchy, for example, attracted Gerry's cynicism, and made him resent the fact that he had to supervise younger children. Marion, on the other hand, totally accepted that same hierarchy and her place within it, but regretted that it was not more efficient. If Gerry had got the effective school council he wanted, it is extremely unlikely that its decisions would reassure Marion, and it is certain that 'crooks' like Pete and Susan would ignore any council's recommendations with cheerful nonchalance.

A kid's past history, too, is always important but does not always carry the same importance. For Gerry, his early career as a lower-school rebel made him a much more wary and wiser critic of education, whereas it was Pete's very success earlier in his school life that was to prove his undoing. Having got used to a pyramidal model of achievement with himself at the top, it was understandably difficult for him to adjust to a different pattern. It might be that public examinations and simply growing up may together enable him to rediscover his talents, but those same public examinations were for Terry a grave disservice. He was always too mature and pleasant to be merely disruptive, but he could surely have been more usefully employed if the decision to stay on at school had not necessarily committed him to a barrage of examinations, most of which he was bound to fail.

Home background, of course, plays a crucial part in most school behaviour, but this again cannot be used as a simple, invariable key to motives and remedies. Of the six kids I have mentioned, one was a virtual mother to her younger brothers and sisters, another had elder brothers and sisters working and married, another came from a very small village, and yet another was the child of a policeman. Each of these factors might make a difference, but in varying directions and to varying extents. Also, each one would take time and tact to discover, and none would provide an easy explanation.

There is not, of course, any reason why we should have explanations or solutions for everything, and it is a lot healthier for us if we do not. What we should have, though, is the concern and curiosity to look for answers, and the recognition that we do not own our pupils. They have a separate, eventful and important life which may not be any of our business but which will spill over the 9-to-4 boundaries which pretend to separate home from school. When that overlap occurs, it may be pitifully inadequate to treat the difficulty as though it were simply a school matter, raised in lesson-time and therefore to be resolved by teacher: 'Susan has not done her Spanish homework: Susan must be punished.'

The conditions in which we work mean that sometimes what we do *is* pitifully inadequate, and quite as soulless as the example above. In a later chapter, in fact, I offer advice which may well seem to recommend a positive programme of such insensitivity. Thus it is as well to begin with the realisation that any child's life must be complex and continually changing. What I see in my lessons will be the tip of an iceberg, and a melting one at that. Few teachers see more of any one kid than four hours a week during term time (that is, less than 170 hours a year), and during all of that time there will be at least twenty-nine others needing that teacher's attention, whether or not they are deliberately seeking it. Within that limited period during which I encounter kids (about 200 of them a week, and I am lucky if it is that few) I may encounter vibrations within any one kid from a whole range of possible sources – the previous lesson, a fight in the play-ground, scandal about a teacher, trouble at home, the death of a pet, being dropped from a team, bad dreams, money lost, a valuable present stolen, a film on TV, a new friendship, trouble imminent or feared. All these, plus mundane arrangements, general pressures and random thoughts will swirl around in the same head which we wish to occupy with lyric poetry or quadratic equations.

A full understanding would involve our finding out about the life of kids beyond our class-room walls, not simply in other subjects and out-of-school activities ('Grand lad, Simpson – best scrum-half I have had in years') but literally out of school. What village, street or estate does each kid live in? What is the family history, present set-up and nature of their difficulties? Who are their friends, in and out of school? How many, and how close? What are their hobbies, tastes and ambitions? How do they spend lunchtimes, evenings, weekends and holidays? What are their feelings about, preferences within and expectations from school? Which memories affect them most powerfully, and why? On paper, in questionnaire form, that list would amount to a gross invasion of privacy, and if we were to simply demand it of kids they would rightly tell us little. It is in such questions, and full, honest answers to them, that the way to understanding lies, but the value of the answers will be determined by who asks the questions, and how; it is also worth noting that kids – like anyone else – value good listeners as well as good talkers. Many kids will welcome a genuine interest in their lives, but it is still necessary for the teacher to remember that he or she sets out as an uninvited guest on dangerous and hallowed ground.

Chapter 4

Contexts of Discipline

'Out of Control' described a riot, where the inexperience of the teacher and the rebellion of his class were clearly the key factors in producing chaos. But there were other considerations which helped that chaos to develop – different material, or a different subject, on a Tuesday morning, might well have produced a less disastrous outcome.

It is the purpose of this chapter to examine these other factors, the contexts of discipline, from which crises of control arise and by which their development is often determined. This can only be an initial framework, but as even that skeleton is currently lacking it seems worth offering a rough outline.

The School Régime

To an individual kid, School may mean a number of things – particular friends, teachers loved, feared or despised, sporting facilities or interesting gossip; the irritations of uniform or homework, the excitement of learning, the constant pressure of compulsion, the fear of being bullied or the chance of an escape from home. To a young teacher, school is money, regular hours, the first full-time job and a territory to explore, exciting or frightening perhaps, but certainly confusing.

In that state of innocence, you cannot be expected to have a clear picture of the lives of your pupils. You do need, though, some sense of the school as a whole and its impact on your charges. More specifically, you need the daily recognition that just as school is only a part of the kids' lives, so you are only a part of school. You are a fleeting moment on the kid's time-table just as he is an occasional entry on yours, and those same classes whose character, behaviour and relationships seem to you so personal and distinctive will also have lessons with other teachers, whose influence on them will be just as great as yours.

The nature and extent of a school régime cannot be simply defined, but it is negatively safe to assume that a comprehensive school cannot have the simple clarity of purpose proclaimed by some selective schools in the past. Single-mindedness as an abstract virtue may be impressive, but it has little relevance for a school of a thousand unselected pupils, any one of whom may need social confidence, academic qualifications, moral awareness, basic skills of literacy, wide-ranging interests, independence, personal integrity or emotional maturity, and each of whom will need these things in different proportions. To select one from such a list of aims as the paramount goal might well make our work simpler, but it would be neither realistic nor efficient.

Generally, if sluggishly, we have come to recognise the limits of selection. A crude division into 'schools for bright kids', 'schools for technical kids' and 'schools for practical kids' will not do justice to the subtle variations between pupils, and will often damage development or waste potential by seeking to force kids into a mould which does not truly fit them. Thus a large, comprehensive school – like an unstreamed class – is not an idealistic pretence that all are the same, but a realistic admission that each is different, and will therefore need large and sensitive resources.

One past consequence of selection was that some schools deliberately created a régime intended to distinguish their members from the ordinary people of the town – caps to be worn, no smoking, chewing gum or ice lollies in public, skirts and hair length to be carefully measured. To accord with such a code, appearance and behaviour must adhere to strictly predetermined limits, which thus clearly and rapidly mark out pupils as belonging to a particular institution, a school apart from the rest, the local community, the mass. With a comprehensive school, however, the mass does not exist; there is no community 'out there' against which the school is to be contrasted, because the school's children are also the town's children. This means that purposeful segregation is neither possible nor desirable, and it also means that responsibility for behaviour (of whatever kind) must be shared between parent, teacher and child.

To me, such a movement towards the integration of the school within the community seems a clear gain, but it does create some short-term problems for both teachers and pupils. A young teacher who was himself educated at a tightly controlled grammar school, where university entrance was an unquestioned achievement, early leaving a crime and Oxbridge scholarships the ultimate goal, might well miss the sense of order which that single purpose was able to instil. Having been carefully rehearsed by his education lecturers in the arguments for a comprehensive system, it might well be disconcerting for him to find that social justice in action sometimes involves noise, frequent movement and numerous faces that he does not and will not ever know.

Few probationary teachers will feel equipped to assess a school régime, and confident generalisation based on two incidents and a misunderstood comment usually turns out to be wrong. Possible pointers, however, include: teachers' view of the school's efficiency, the annual turnover of staff, the atmosphere in the staff-room (and the variations between different areas of it), the nature of the teaching hierarchy and the communication between different levels thereof, the feelings of local residents and parents, the ages and social background of both teachers and parents, the school's recent history and future plans and – most important and elusive of all – the demeanour of kids, in and out of lessons.

To the kids themselves, the clearest expression of the school régime is not morning assembly or speech day, but rules. These are usually negative and ideally rational, but few schools could honestly claim reason as the sole motivation for every restriction they apply. The very seriousness of that application is also quite as variable as the underlying motivation; some are allowed to drift happily into disuse, while others are tenaciously applied long after they have ceased to perform any useful function.

For the individual teacher, a compulsory rule which is generally enforced can present some tricky dilemmas. I once had a very tough third-year group with whom survival was a necessary aim, and fruitful work an occasional and impressive achievement. My struggles were complicated by the headmaster's invariable requirement that each teacher of English should set two homeworks to each class every week. For me at that time, with that class, I could see no way of making this a positive arrangement; those who wanted to borrow books to read, or who wished to write stories in privacy, did so anyway, and on the few occasions when I set compulsory homeworks I spent so much time in lessons chasing up exercise books that it would have been better if I had not bothered. In the end I kept all exercise books in the room, carefully collecting each one before the end of the lesson, and set virtually no homework; this meant that I defied the school rule, but the kids did a lot more work and I was both happier and more efficient.

This is an extreme example, where a difficult, streamed class and the absence of staff consultation pushed me into a nasty choice, between the needs of the school régime and the needs of my own teaching. The fact that I chose the latter in this particular case does not mean, of course, that I would always decide that way, and in many schools the realism and intelligence of senior staff would make such a decision unnecessary. Where the dilemma is insoluble, however, I would offer the risky principle that teacher survival matters more than headmaster approval; if it is a question of basic effectiveness – rather than a personal preference or whim – then the chances are that thirty kids can inflict more discomfort than one headmaster, and you will certainly spend more time with them than you will with him.

So far as the kids are concerned, only time will tell you which rules matter, or how thoroughly or consistently they are enforced. The worst situation is that where there are some rules which some staff ignore but which other staff rigorously apply, so that it can be a difficult, costly lesson finding out who observes what. If only to give yourself some useful background information, and also to guard against the inevitable 'Honest, sir, I thought we were allowed to smoke', you need to find out which rules exist, and how widely and effectively they are enforced.

Honest answers to such questions will not always come from the TES advert or the headmaster's interview, but you will need as soon as possible some picture of the school's régime and the extent to which it impinges on kids' lives and thereby (however perversely) affects their attitudes. As a young teacher, you will probably not be consulted about this régime, but you will be expected in some sense to maintain it and it will already have been in force for the kids you teach long before you arrive on the scene, so it may save you from some obvious blunders to find out something of your teaching context before you close your class-room door.

Subjects and Departments

Once inside, you will face a period of time which in your time-table and your mind is labelled Physics, History or Car Mechanics. The label will not worry you, since you have spent some time thinking about it as your speciality, and have probably got some certificate to testify how much you knew about it on the day of an exam. Certainly, you will have a more advanced knowledge of it than most of your pupils, since the bulk of them will be below 'O' level standard, and your own interest and talent probably flowered rather later than your sixteenth birthday.

So far as discipline is concerned, your subject is important, but not for the philosophical reason that you are 'an authority' as well as 'in authority'; whatever the expectations of professional intellectuals, academic expertise is a dubious foundation on which to base your claim to control. More practically, different subjects have distinctive disciplinary needs, about which student teachers need to be better informed.

Craft, for instance, is usually taught in workshops by men who give decisive orders, expect rapid obedience and are very strict when they do not get it. The reasons for this are partly traditional, in that these men have themselves been taught by stern craftsmen (and have in many cases experienced a much cruder discipline in industry), but partly rational. For while it may be sensitive and liberating to encourage a child to experiment with adjectives or a lump of clay, the same does not apply to an electric drill or guillotine.

A rockface, language laboratory and a poisonous gas each present unique disciplinary problems, and it is obviously up to teachers in each area to determine their own needs for class control as well as for teaching method and equipment. It is vital, however, that rational grounds for caution should not become the basis for a less rational authority, so that 'You cannot do anything you want because it might be dangerous' hardens into 'You do that now because I tell you'. It should still be possible to take sensible precautions and yet be concerned for exploration and relevant choice; drama teachers, often ridiculed as the ethereal dreamers of the teaching world, must spend their time both safeguarding valuable equipment and encouraging kids to think their own thoughts and decide their own movements. The intelligent practice of discipline excludes neither freedom nor common sense.

Within the subject area, the type of work required is also a factor. Some assignments will be clear, simply defined and easily marked, offering students a long series of short tasks to be completed in succession. Other work may be far less definite, spreading over a longer period and offering a number of possible 'correct' solutions. Both these extremes carry their own disciplinary risks: kids can become bored with repetition, depressed by failure and insulted by simplicity; but they can also be bewildered by choice, frightened by open-ended questions and made restless by long periods of time without fresh stimulus.

In this respect the modern revolution in teaching aims and methods directly affects discipline. If the aim is instruction, indoctrination or demonstration, it is enough to demand that kids sit still and shut up. That is a simple, if sometimes unattainable, objective, because it is unambiguous; kids know what you want, and you know when they are stopping you from getting it. If, on the other hand, you want kids to say what they think, criticise another point of view or relate an idea to something they know well, traditional discipline will actively destroy what you are trying to create. Encouraging kids to talk and think their own thoughts (rather than simply to reproduce an authority's opinion) produces a whole new range of unavoidable problems and delicate decisions with which our forbears were never faced, and which we have to accept as the price of real progress.

But work has not 'gone democratic', from one simple pattern to another. In English, there are times when I want a lot of people talking (group discussions, play preparation), times when I want one person talking (reading a story aloud, play performances), times when I want general quiet with occasional chatter (writing poems), and times when I want total hush (individual reading). This is a complex set of demands for one teacher to make of his class, and it necessarily allows more room for misunderstanding and exploitation than a single inflexible rule.

Your choice of work, therefore, should be governed by the disciplinary situation as well as by the demands of the syllabus or the logical structure of your subject. The obvious next step – doing the following chapter, finishing off that story you started last week or completing that stage of the course – may all look reasonable enough in the solitary calm of preparation, but you need also to think how such activities will look to those kids in that lesson at that time.

This assumes, perhaps too optimistically, that you have control over your teaching material, and it is here that your membership of a department becomes relevant. The precise meaning of the term 'department' varies between subjects and between schools, and the impact of a department on its probationary teachers can vary alarmingly from obstruction to dictatorship. Personally, I have been lucky to have worked in departments where teachers were given an entirely free hand as to how they spent their lesson time. Books were offered and advice was on hand, but nothing was 'set' for the teacher. Others will not be so lucky, or may find that the cost and effort of producing their own materials (even if they are allowed to use them) is prohibitive in terms of energy and time. Worse still, there is little incentive to cure disciplinary problems when the material which may aggravate them is beyond the teacher's control. I can still hear the bitter cry of a student teacher haranguing her maths group – 'It's not my fault you've got to do this; I've been told to do it, so get on with it!'

Such compulsion can create insoluble problems. The low-stream class, compelled to follow a syllabus they dislike for an examination they will fail in a subject they despise, will make their protest felt, and not through a coolly argued memorandum to the headmaster. Teachers on the receiving end of such resentment will understandably feel helpless if they have no control over the work they are supposed to initiate. Worse still, probationers who are the victims of such arrangements usually lack the objectivity to define the roots of the problem, and thus blame themselves for anything which falls short of ideal teaching. A close, clear look at the context of their work should at least free these potential casualties of the feeling that they are responsible for everything which goes wrong. For some faults they may well be to blame, and guilt is helpful if it enables them to correct those and improve, but when the crucial decisions have been made elsewhere it has no place. You will be busy enough trying to salvage something from the fiasco without indulging in the luxury of irrelevant self-criticism.

Short of such depressing situations, it is also worth knowing in outline the history of your own department within the school. The fact that you are the eighth maths teacher to arrive in two years, or the knowledge that they had a marvellous Spanish department which left *en bloc* last summer, will not make you teach differently but might help to explain your impact on kids. You cannot change the past, but knowing about it will help you to set yourself realistic targets. The obvious source of information (the kids who have been there longer than you) should be discreetly and gradually tapped, making allowance for the usual exaggerations – 'We never did anything with Mr Harris' might mean what it says, or might mean that Mr Harris was a very cunning teacher who had mastered the knack of providing painless work.

Such inquiries will occasionally tell you exactly what you need to know – that this form have always had Miss Johnson, who was marvellous, and they are holding that against you; or that English until three weeks ago meant weekly spelling tests and dictations; or that they have never done any oral French, or drama, or experiments; or that Mr Black never set them any homework so you will have to work hard to get any back. None of this information will provide an ideal slot into which, chameleon-like, you can fit, but it does tell you something about the territory onto which you are treading, and understanding – although it will not always get you out of trouble – will usually do more good than harm.

Time-Table, Furniture and Equipment

The syllabus may be great, the subject matter inspiring and the head of department out of this world, but if the time-table has it in for you life will still be very hard.

Firstly, time of day. Some kids dread morning lessons because lunch seems a long way off, and like the afternoon because it is nearly time to go home, but teachers seldom agree. A class that is angelic at 9.30 a.m. can be restive by 2.00 p.m. and positively murderous by 3.30 p.m. Double lessons in the afternoon can seem endless and often require at least two separate activities; you may not need one of them if you are lucky, but you will be glad to have it in reserve.

The comprehensive time-table is so complicated that if the thing comes out at all everyone is delighted, and no one can afford to consider how the results may affect the individual teacher. In my first year of teaching, for instance, I had four of my five 'free' periods on a Thursday, and the three classes which caused me most trouble all visited my room on a Friday afternoon. Every weekend for an entire school year started with a 4 o'clock shadow, and preparation and marking began in exhaustion and gloom.

Place is as important as time. Again I have been lucky, with a teaching base of my own throughout my career, in which I have been free to keep exercise books, text books and odd bits of material, flourishing in a chaotic but fecund pile of intellectual manure. If you can secure a home territory of your own, and can manage to give it something of a personal flavour which will cheer you up and survive the regular impact of kids, this can be both a practical and a psychological help.

If, on the other hand, you are less fortunate, and have to commute vast distances between rooms, carrying what you require from staff-room to teaching-room and back again, you'll have to pick up very quickly a tight routine for checking teaching aids, exercise books and so on. If, as sometimes happens, you are not sure where a lesson is meant to be held, try to find out beforehand, as there are few more harrowing experiences than being a new teacher leading an experienced class in search of a room they might not want to find.

Within the room, one of the crucial factors is the arrangement of furniture. This may sound trivial, but it can be decisive, and you would be well advised to think about what you want before you find out the hard way that you have not got it. Also, you do not have to be bound by the habits of other teachers who use the room, although you will have to organise your kids to leave the furniture as it was when you came in – or even neater.

Personally, I like working with tables arranged in about half a dozen blocks, but although such an arrangement gets approving nods from visiting lecturers I would not advise it to teachers who are not happy with it; if you are not sure, wait. In the first place, kids are badly situated for listening to you, and you may have to establish an awkward routine of having them turn their chairs round when you want to talk to the group as a whole. Secondly, the price of having compatible groups who have chosen to sit together is that a lot of gossip gets talked, and it is far harder for the teacher, who is physically outside the circle of conversation, to control the volume of chat, check on its relevance to the work or identify the author of any sudden disturbance.

For anyone uncertain of their control over a particular class, it is easier to have parallel lines or a two-tiered U shape (with all desks facing the teacher's, between the arms of the U); for those in dire trouble, there is no substitute for the pairs routine, with clearly defined corridors and everyone facing the front. That way, any crossing of boundaries, whether physical or verbal, is more obvious and requires more nerve, and you have the additional option of standing at the back watching them without them staring at you. Education, of course, is a different matter, but if you are in dire trouble you will not be too immediately concerned with education.

School record-players, tape-recorders and cassettes (as well as chalk and board rubbers) are frequently used and often go missing, so it is worth knowing what is available, in working order and how you can go about getting it. Looking at the department record-player the previous day is not enough if by the time the lesson has come round someone has taken it, your record has been borrowed or you have not got a power-point in the room. Similarly, if you get a mid-lesson inspiration that now would be a good time to do some taping, do not send eight kids scouring the school for a tape-recorder; other staff will not thank you for interrupting their lessons and you should have booked it or fetched it before.

This cannot be an exhaustive analysis. Outside the class-room possibilities are endless, as breaks, lunchtimes and 4 o'clock combine to throw up a succession of incidents, any one of which can escalate into crisis. The first and last time I caned a boy resulted from a silly, unnecessary confrontation which occurred when I paid a hurried impulse visit to a friend in another house during a hectic afternoon break. Only this week I became involved in a fierce argument with a kid I had never met before through the sheer accident of my happening to return a record-player to a distant room at 4.05 p.m. instead of later.

Over your whole school week, you will be forced to make all sorts of decisions that have little to do with teaching, but which may be vital to your effectiveness within the school. In addition to your room and your lessons, you may also have to decide how much you mind about table manners, jostling in passages or bubble gum, and choose whether you are going to do anything about swearing, lateness or smoking at the bus stop. Neither this nor any other book can give you an exhaustive summary of what to expect, or a list of infallible responses, but this brief outline does at least suggest some basic factors which will affect your regular dealings with your classes.

Chapter 5

The Teacher's Job

The teacher, because he is the one adult in the class-room, is sometimes expected to be both omnipotent and universally flexible. Some educational writing, which outlines 'the needs of the children' and then goes on to define what teachers should be like, implies that we are made of Meccano, to be built up and manipulated in whatever direction seems best. But teachers, like their pupils, are individuals with rights and should be no more subject to impossible demands than their charges. We cannot be endlessly kind, totally accepting or entirely committed just because it might make schools nicer if we were; like children and anyone else, we must start from where we are.

For the young teacher, this means ruthless self-awareness. You may well be self-conscious enough already, trying to adopt a prominent role you are not sure of, but self-awareness is a lot more precise. What sort of person are you – confident, shy, efficient, disorganised, enthusiastic or steady? What kinds of atmosphere do you work best in – busy, intense, ordered or sleepy? What do you do best, and what has that to do with the kids you will teach? Honest answers to such questions may or may not tell you the sort of teacher you will become, but they will certainly help you to set realistic goals which take your own personality into account, making allowance both for talents and for limitations.

Physically, if you happen to have a 6-foot frame and a booming voice, that is part of your equipment you may be glad of. But if you are 5-foot 2 inches and squeak it is not the end of the world; you simply have to find approaches which will use what you have got, and stay clear of stand-up confrontations.

Your clothes may matter, too. Even if the choice is entirely yours, it is worth making with pupils in mind. Will the clothes you feel best in attract comment from them, and if so, do you mind? A man's long hair may reflect his personal liberation, but will he tire of being called Jesus? People have lost jobs through less, and though pettiness and custom need not terrorise you into drab conformity, it is worth thinking about the immediate image you present, so that the first casual comments do not break your heart.

Teachers also import into school their own assumptions about the basic concepts of 'school', 'authority' and 'work', powerfully influenced by their own schooling. As yet there are very few teachers in comprehensive schools who themselves attended comprehensive schools; by far the majority have been through some form of selective process, which will have conditioned their idea of what 'teaching' means. They may be passionate élitists, convinced of the value of the competition which has stretched them, or democrats outraged by the divisive strain their rise has caused, but no one starts work as a teacher entirely neutral. If you have come from an academic background of some kind, it is probable that the impact of a comprehensive will change your views in some direction (although it is impossible to predict precisely), so you might as well be clear what they are to start with.

Once the work of teaching starts, you become subject to a series of demands. The private life for which you have decreasing energy and time will affect your teaching life, and a string of apparently irrelevant events may contribute to class-room disasters – a friend dropping in for a drink, travelling problems, love affairs, the menstrual cycle or car trouble. Everything combines to eat into your life, eroding the brittle base of confidence on which your teaching precariously rests. As a result it is often tempting to live near the school and pour everything into your teaching life, although if that fails you have nothing left for consolation. But whatever the individual decisions you have to make, you need to think about where and how you live, how you are going to get into school, what else you want to do with your time and what you might give up if you had to. Your first year in teaching can make frightening demands, and although you will not get a divorce to make yourself a better teacher, it is worth seeing how you can arrange your outside life to cushion the blows to come. Do not, for instance, live with mum thirty miles away just because you think she might like it – by the time you have got home, done two lots of marking and prepared eight lessons you will be no use to her or anyone else.

As the prospect of action looms nearer, it is only natural to spend some time thinking about what sort of teacher you want to be; most of us have our own heroes from our educational past, who in some way we would like to resemble, and negative examples can be just as powerfully effective – 'I may not be much good, but I shall not end up like *her*!' It is certainly useful to raid the past for hints and specific memories, but they will not be sufficient.

Most teachers have been successful in the educational system. They may not have been angels (and like everyone else they will exaggerate their own teenage behaviour in retrospect), but they were bright enough to be interested and successful in the work that was given them, and they were probably taught in schools more tightly regimented than today's comprehensives. In discipline terms, therefore, the past may be an inappropriate guide; the Welsh PE master who frightened me might not frighten the kids I teach today, because they are tougher than I was and whole patterns of behaviour have changed. It is therefore not worth my while trying to control a difficult kid in the way that he would have done.

Another inadequate source of enlightenment is the work of one's colleagues. In my first year I used regularly to torture myself by eavesdropping on the wise old men who controlled my worst classes with the flick of an eyelid. 'Robinson?' they would remark calmly, of my worst problem, 'he's no bother', and I would quietly shrink another 6 inches. Even when I moved to another school, and could handle all the kids I taught bar two, I was jealous of two members of staff who had no trouble with them. They were both around my age, did not seem exceptionally gifted or ferocious, so what was I doing wrong?

All I was doing wrong was looking for perfection. One of these teachers had taught my *bête noire* for a year before I came, and so could meet him cheerily in a corridor, have a violent mock fight and then depart whistling while I marvelled at his nerve. The other had power simply because he was expert in a subject important to the boy concerned – he would do what he was told by an engineer who knew about cars, but why should he listen to an English teacher when he himself could barely read and did not want to learn? That kind of discipline depends on personalities, and we all have our limits; if I had thought about it, there were kids I taught well who had got less from either of those teachers, but when you feel you are failing you often do not think that clearly.

There is no sense, and a lot of grief, in an inexperienced teacher comparing himself with an experienced one, for at least three reasons: (1) unless the latter is totally stupid, he must have learned *something* from his experience – and that gives him an advantage; (2) a kid is more likely to obey you when he knows you, particularly if you have taught him when he is 11 or 12; (3) you are presumably going to get better as you go on, which means that your present incompetent state is only temporary, part of a learning process. That being so, it is silly to pass a damning judgement on your ability before you have started.

This does not mean it is not worth watching other teachers and talking with them about their work; it is, and it is one of the quickest ways to get better, as long as you do not let irrelevancies like jealousy or guilt get in the way. In six years I have taught with a colossal range of staff, and the most valuable thing they have taught me is the futility of simple models; I started out with a vague but inspiring picture of the 'ideal teacher', whom I would imagine, perhaps meet and then observe and even finally, to the sound of trumpets, become. That picture has been torn up, not because superb teaching is impossible, but because it is so variously possible that it eludes definition.

Many of the teachers I have admired have been quite different from one another, and most of them possess qualities which in them are virtues but which I would not want for myself. One was a traditional sec. mod. maths teacher on the verge of retirement, strict, cheerful and obscenely witty in private, who knew his local area like the back of his hand; another was a girl teaching RE, confidently holding beliefs I disagreed with violently, but involving the entire range of secondary kids in all kinds of activities, which they enjoyed and learned from, and from which the whole school gained; there was a Cambridge graduate, quietly wise, who through patience, trust and application earned the affectionate respect of delinquents, university entrants and all his colleagues; or the drama teacher, uniquely self-effacing, who could have blasted kids into worshipful submission but preferred to talk with them instead. None of these would have seemed impressive during my period of training, and none of them is exactly the kind of teacher I think I want to be, but they are all doing the job well and because of that I have learned from each of them.

The word 'job', in that last sentence and in the title of this chapter, is deliberate. It suggests an unromantic slog, something for which you are paid because it has to be done and you need the money. This is not the traditional view of the teacher's role, and it does not exclude the sheer enjoyment or 'professional status' so revered by the unions, but it sometimes needs asserting against the airier descriptions of classroom action:

'He confronts the class. He looks happy and "at home". Let him cherish his merry twinkle and keep ever green his quality of pleasantness. Let him cherish too the quality of sympathy to which even the most unresponsive of pupils will succumb. . . .'[1]

A teacher is not simply a jolly amateur displaying ideal virtues; he works for a living and consequently has to do some things he does not want to do. More important, he has to relate his personal qualities

[1] Davies and Shepherd, *Teaching: Begin Here* (Epworth, 1949; rev. edn. 1961), p. 61.

to the world in which he works, and its pace and complexity ensure that simple dedication and kindness are not enough. The qualities which mark out the most effective teachers seem to me less absolute but closely relevant to the conditions of work. They are:

(a) Flexibility: they adapt their response to kids and situations, retaining the capacity for great firmness when necessary.

(b) Sensitivity: the standards and aims they set are related to the kids they teach; these may seem surprisingly low or high, but they are the targets of people who continue to teach.

(c) Timing: they allow a shy kid half a term before they make a direct comment which might seem threatening, but nip potential riots in the bud before kids are aware that they might start.

(d) Sense of proportion: they know when situations, kids or they themselves are ridiculous, will admit it, laugh at it, and then get on with the job.

(e) Relaxation: they find a rhythm in which they are happy, do not perform flat out from 9 till 4, and because of that their classes feel secure, and often do not consider mucking about.

(f) Reserve: they hold something back for real crises; an extrovert may become ominously quiet, or a patient soft-spoken pedagogue may erupt in sudden anger. In either case, kids recognise something new, and do not feel they have exhausted the teacher's resources.

These are not absolute virtues, but they are qualities that work, in obtaining humane control and encouraging stable relationships. They are a purely personal list, and other teachers could easily work out their own, quite different but equally valid. What matters, though, is that the list should relate to the conditions of the job, rather than being derived from an abstract scale of values, flattering self-image or nostalgia for a misremembered past. Anyone hoping to recapture the aura of Thomas Arnold in a modern comprehensive will fail, not because youth has gone to the dogs and standards have declined, but because Thomas Arnold did not teach mixed-ability groups for thirty-five lessons a week.

For someone who has not taught, it may be difficult to imagine precisely what these conditions are, and it is obviously true that in one sense every single teacher operates in a unique situation. On the other hand, there are recurrent factors, and it is important that as much knowledge as possible be shared among prospective teachers, so that they start out with at least some knowledge of what to expect. Simply as information, therefore, I offer a diary of one day from my own teaching week. I chose the day in advance, without knowing what might come up, and it is certainly not intended to represent an extreme or an ideal. So far as discipline is concerned, it contains only one serious situation, but it does show the surrounding context from which such crises emerge, and within which they have to be resolved. Consistently throughout the day, you have to make a number of decisions, some of them disciplinary, and you never know in advance exactly which decisions may prove to be decisive.

The Teacher's Day

8.50 Arrive, collect daily bulletin and messages from pigeon hole. See two members of staff about forthcoming house pantomime.

8.55 Collect register, go to tutor set, read out daily announcements, check on dinner numbers and notes from previous day's absentees. Pass on a mild complaint to Mary about messing about in the library – not a long sermon, just enough to let her know I am in touch with the librarian.

Then send Martin to fetch Bill from his tutor set, so I can see them both about disrupting Miss Harvey's lesson on Tuesday. She is very keen to find some positive solution, wants to know what they think and does not want me to drop on them from a height. Interesting chat; they have serious misconceptions (such as, that she despises their slowness – utterly wrong, as I think I have convinced them) and also make revealing comments on pattern of her lessons, which do not offer them much. Their account of the trouble they caused is predictably milder than hers, but hammering that inconsistency now would shut them up.

9.25 Dismiss tutor set, stuck for what to do with fifth year 'O' level and CSE group; a timed essay would be lazy – they have done a few and will do a lot more later. Borrow play set, conveniently taken out of county library by colleague who does not need it this lesson.

Start by asking for 'My Last Duchess' essay, due in though I had nearly forgotten it. Only one handed in. Throw small, controlled fit, stressing the freedom they have had to organise their own work and abuse of deadline (*Q*: should I have allowed the freedom?). Go round whole group, one at a time, asking for reasons why not done; none very convincing, all a bit shamefaced, by the end I am almost amused but dare not admit it; quick end to lecture, dire threat about consequences of not doing it tomorrow – then rapid change of key, pleasant hour's play-reading.

10.40 Fifteen minutes' break, effectively cut to ten, after I have chatted to Carol about how nice it is to do plays, travelled to the staff-room and queued for my coffee. Also have to catch two other house staff about pantomime, so no real rest.

10.50 'Free' lesson goes, substituting for absent French teacher. Luckily work is set, I look fierce and remote for five minutes and get on with the marking I need to get done before afternoon lessons.

11.25 Third year, regular silent reading lesson. Once they have settled down (and they are used to the routine) I am free to tidy my room with minimal attention to kids (most of whom are in any case happily in their own worlds). With a couple I need to ask what they are reading, what page they are on, what it is about, etc., and then ask again five minutes later, but generally it is easy.

12.00 Peaceful lesson finishes peacefully. Kids rush to dinner, I rush to supervise house swimming. Must be there quickly to ensure that kids are not swimming unsupervised (legally dangerous); also to check on invited visitors from other houses. No problems as long as you make a habit of being there early. Half an hour ambling round pool, trying not to be deafened or splashed.

12.30 Clear kids out of pool – shout once, then walk slowly down from far end towards changing rooms, getting them to clear up rings etc. as they go; then get them to dress themselves – another shift due in and they will miss their lunch if they are not quick.

12.40 Go to own class-room to collect lunch and marking. Discover small meeting in progress (remedial specialist reporting back after 'underprivileged children' course) for which I cannot spare the time, unfortunately. Quietly intrude, pick up books and food, and go else-where to mark and munch. Bump into Miss Harvey, pass on the relevant bits of the morning's chat with Martin and Bill.

1.20 Collect register, walk to tutor set room, tick off who is there, and then return to teaching-room to check all is ready.

1.30 Arrival of 4B – their second year of me and my sixth year of teaching, but a lively proposition nonetheless. Stan is shouting, Mary turning round as soon as I open my mouth, and Jon singing tunelessly. They are not trained to instant obedience, but I can get bursts of silence when I want them. I get one for long enough to explain what is wanted – each pick one of Ulster press photos on wall as basis for a story (key requirement: try to make it *real* – think about people as well as actions). Later, those who want a closer look at the photos can get it, but not straight away; get as many started as soon as possible. Thanks to determination, ready pile of marked books and spare pens (note each one issued) we start better than usual and within five minutes I am free to wander round offering individual assistance.

This made easier by my desk arrangement – six blocks, as at junior schools, with friends together and more space between and around tables; this means I can move round more freely, although there is at least one group I may have to break up; not a crisis today, but bear it in mind for later. Might be best, too, to warn them of the possibility while I am calm, rather than waiting till I have had too much and will not be quite so rational.

Going round, I find Sally's done nothing, so I casually suggest that she does it tomorrow lunchtime (*thinks*: am I free? Who is her tutor? Will she come? When do I teach them next if she does not?). She is angry at the suggestion, so luckily it is enough to mobilise her briefly. As kids finish, I encourage them to move on to their own reading, but that is not always easy. Gillian sulks because I have forgotten the horse book I promised her, and Jon and Reg, who have done all the writing they can usefully do, can read very little. Time-saving, I lend them my own copy of a book of photographs, which keeps them busy without boosting their literacy.

Kevin, as usual, has finished early, and added the bits I asked for when commenting on his first effort; I cannot ask for more, but he is not going in the library as he suggests, because on past evidence he will resist anything except temptation, and the library offers too much. I ignore his 'There aren't any good books here', since my brusque 'What sort of book do you want then?' gets only a casual 'Dunno'. In ten minutes, going over possible library books, I might get somewhere, but today that sort of time is not available.

For once Mary is working well, and I dare not endanger that. Showing vast enthusiasm before she is finished would stop her immediately, so I build a cocoon around her, shutting up the friends who might distract her, since her own distraction potential is so vast. She is busy for a quarter of an hour at a time, and that is a gain.

As I wander, I notice Mike tearing up bits of paper and spreading them carefully over the floor. I quietly inform him that he is tidying the room at the end of the lesson – he has become very devious recently and sharply ironical; if I lectured or interrogated him now I would lose.

Viv, chatty, friendly and intelligent at her best, is today exasperating. Luckily for me, I call her over instead of simply yelling 'Viv, shut up'; she explains, happily and without preamble, that her mum and dad are splitting up and she is relieved. Not for me to comment, but she is happier for having told her news, and therefore will accept my pointing out that she is distracting others.

By the end of the double it has been a pleasant session, some good work done and no outbursts. Now only break and two singles to go, and I cannily get everything packed up and tidied away so that when the bell goes we can all have a full break – all luxurious ten minutes of it.

2.40 The bell goes, I am happy and everyone has gone except Mike, obediently and placidly picking up bits of paper, and Stan – who just has to interrupt the final seconds of peace by releasing the window blinds.

These blinds cover the window tastefully enough but are controlled by long strings which wrap conveniently round chair legs, so that through careful arrangement you can make other people lower the blind dramatically as soon as they move their chairs. Stan has done this before in the lesson, and been warned off it, so I have got to do something. I decide to be petty, and make him lower and raise each of the four blinds, to show that he knows how to do it and to make him look faintly stupid. That will take long enough to irritate him but not so long that I miss my tea.

Duly irritated, he does each one, slowly and satirically, but gives the last a spectacular yank which threatens to break the entire mechanism. My move. Trying not to scream, punch or give up, I placidly tell him to raise the blinds he has lowered, and then go through it again; he needs the practice and sir is boss. He does not agree, refuses, and escalation is under way.

Being harassed and fed up, I decide to invoke help. So long as I do not hit him I can claim straight disobedience on two counts (ignoring warning, refusing order) and pass the buck to someone else with status and time; his house master is away, but the Head's obliging about being used occasionally as an instant figurehead. Stan gets one more chance to do the blinds, but by now he wants to go the whole way, so off we go. The boss is out preparing for assembly, but luckily I meet the deputy house master who just happens to teach Stan the next lesson and he agrees to say the appropriate words.

2.50 Bell goes as I take my first sip of tea. Cool it from the tap, down the lot, grab books from my room *en route* for my next performance, with 4A, some way away. The lesson is mediocre but uneventful, and gives me a little time to work out what I will say to Stan.

3.25 Last lesson, and our crazy time-table gives me 4B again. There is an emergency school assembly at 3.40, so there are effectively ten minutes to kill. Concentrate on Stan, repeat that I want him to raise the blinds. He is uncertain, but does not want to give in any more than I do; luckily for us both, some girls relieve the pressure by tidying up the blinds for him. This does not resolve the battle of wills, but it gets us out of the impasse. I explain why he has not seen the Head, and then string together recent crimes in an indictment, with his defiance making an effective climax. This wholly negative approach ('Look what I've got on you') obscures my weakness by going onto the attack, but will not change a thing. I have made the whole business wearing and petty enough for him to be tired of it too, so he is not actually triumphant. As far as real progress is concerned, I will just have to wait for another time.

3.35 Assembly in the vast sports hall. One of my tutor set is told off for nattering by the deputy head, when I should have seen him first. The Head then addresses us about thefts in the village, the local reputation of the school and the way crime harms each one of us. I silently wonder (*a*) how far that is true, (*b*) who will listen, even if it is, and (*c*) how harmful is the wedge he is trying to drive between the responsible and the crooks. But this is not the time for dissent; he is doing his impossible job better than I am doing mine, so I keep quiet and wait for it to finish.

4.00 At last. But there is a voluntary meeting about a parents' evening (on sex education); I am interested, and worried that it might be taken over by dogmatists, so I go.

By the time I get home at 6.00 p.m. I shall have to be thinking about eight lessons for the next day. I do not teach Stan again till

Monday, but there is nothing I can usefully do or demand which will justify turning tomorrow upside down. There are other things to worry about, like lesson preparation, marking and continuous assessment sheets, as well as a whole series of instantaneous decisions like the ones I have been making all day.

This is a personal record, and in one sense cannot be typical. Not even its worst enemies would call 4B an 'average' class, and I would not always have a free period taken with substitution, be on swimming duty or be drawn to a voluntary meeting. But then I do not always have a free period (three days out of five I teach eight lessons) and on other days I might well have had a department meeting, a house or dinner duty or some sporting commitment. Also, this was an easy teaching morning, with a lucky break to begin with and two virtually silent lessons requiring little effort, and that does not happen every day.

This is, too, the day of a teacher who has been going six years and enjoys his work. For a probationer having a rough time, the day would be just as full, except that the confrontation with Stan might happen every lesson, or might happen with a group of kids, or with four individuals in the same lesson. Instead of the weary cynicism into which I retreated, there might be rising despair, and a cumulative rhythm of misery throughout the day. The physical effort, pace of events and absence of guaranteed rest all make the job extremely tiring, and must affect the whole way you take decisions. It is not simply that you have not time to do what you want; you do not always have time to think what you want to do. My final challenge to Stan, for instance, was brute reflex, violent reaction to pressure and provocation; I knew I could not ignore the blind, silly as it was, because the next exploration would have been more dramatic still, so I relied on sheer power and my instinct for self-preservation. Given more time, I would approach it differently; keep Stan behind, ask him about the blind, remind him that I had told him about it before. With patient questioning, he would have to say more about what he was doing and why, and either admit that it was a daft and avoidable diversion, or else talk about what made it necessary. In the time given, though, that could not have been done meaningfully; him sliding out of the door muttering 'Yes, sir, I am sorry sir, it was very silly, sir, and it will not happen again, sir' would have been just as big a defeat for me as what actually happened, because within the limits of my lesson he has defied me and then escaped unscathed. I do not want him physically 'scathed', but I do want to encroach into his life sufficiently to make him think, and to nudge him out of the complacency of thinking he can do entirely as impulse dictates.

This is not an objective study of levels of misbehaviour; necessarily, I concentrate on the things that go wrong, because those are most urgent and worrying, and I have no way of telling how far this account reflects the experience of other teachers. It is written, though, not to demonstrate the evil of modern kids, but to outline the importance of time for teachers, and that is universal. If I had a guaranteed free lesson to prepare for 4B each time I taught them, I would probably do them something like justice. I would bring Gillian her horse book, find Jon and Reg something that they could read, and I would not feel obliged to try and sort Stan out within five minutes. But after six years of chasing my tail I know that I cannot do a perfect job with one class without doing savage injustice to another. The conditions of work make it simply impossible to spend the time ideally required for preparation and recording, let alone for discipline.

This also applies outside the class-room. If a teacher has just spent five minutes of a break going over a difficult problem with an interested kid, and is belatedly going for his coffee, he does not really want to encounter two little boys fighting in a corridor. If he does, he will either ignore them or simply shout 'Stop that!' firmly enough for them to stop while he is actually going past. He might, of course, ask each one what they were fighting about and why, and arbitrate between them so as to establish peaceful coexistence, but his decision to do that will depend much more on his next lesson and the state of his throat than on his educational philosophy.

The difference between a sensitive teacher and an autocrat is time; the sensitive teacher has time to ask questions, listen to answers and think about solutions, whereas the autocrat wants an answer inside two minutes. There are natural tyrants, who would be curtly destructive whatever the conditions, but you cannot simply shoot them or wait for them to die. For most of us, the understanding impulse is there, but we are not always free to follow it. For example, if a worried little girl comes up to me in a crowded corridor I might say 'What can I do for you?' and I might say 'Not now, love', but I will think of myself as well as her when I decide.

Teacher-time is vital currency, and when you spend a lot of it on stray individuals or optional extras you may find you have none left for an emergency – in your own class-room, with a class you cannot choose to ignore. The little girl in the corridor might need urgent help or she might not; either way, it will be important to her so she will

sound desperate. But you know for certain what you need to do for
your lessons, and it may well be better to work on them and pass the
girl on to someone else.

Such decisions crop up all the time. In lesson 3 of my 'Teacher's
Day', for instance, I supervised another teacher's class. I could have
chosen to sit cheerily on the edge of the desk, chat to the kids and
show off my appalling French accent, and then go round helping them
with their work. In fact, I needed to mark some books for an afternoon lesson, so I spent the minimum time settling down the French
class, which meant being impersonal and probably appearing unsympathetic. Perhaps I should have done 4B's marking the previous
night, but the previous night I was out enjoying myself, and I matter
too.

For the probationer, teacher-time is vital. You need it to talk to
kids, ask questions, check up on excuses and alibis, chase up work
and enforce punishments, and if you have no time to do any of these
your life will be hell. There will be other demands on your time: you
will be a member of a house and department, both of which will have
meetings; you will be a tutor or form-teacher, take part in out-of-
school activities and run a private life of your own, as well as trying
to mark and prepare. You will have to fill in reports, mark internal
exams, attend parents' evenings and full staff meetings. Nor will life
get much easier: with ROSLA, the expansion of CSE Mode 3, the wider
introduction of mixed-ability classes and team-teaching, the growth
of the general sixth and the cultivation of the community school, it
seems likely that education will become more diverse, sensitive and
interesting, and twice as much work for the teachers.

Because of this, you need to watch yourself carefully, particularly
if you are naturally generous and active. In any large school, as in any
town, village or factory, a mixed community throws up hordes of
little incidents which in an ideal world demand attention – kids out of
bounds, wanting to borrow money, trying to pick a fight, being bullied,
looking for somewhere to smoke, or writing graffiti about favourite
teachers. Where the school is a genuine community these incidents
are shared between staff, and you can deal with one thoroughly because
you know someone else will look after the others. Where there is no
sharing, on the other hand, there is a real danger that a few trusting,
sensitive souls will try to do it all. You do not and should not walk
by on the other side every time, but you do owe it to the kids you
teach, and to yourself, to be reasonably prepared and alive, and this
will sometimes mean saying 'No' even to the most appealing kids.

Character and Control

That last piece of advice will sound more calculating than many teachers want to be, and may aggravate existing worries about what teaching may do to you. To hoard your time like a miser may seem mean when there are kids in need of help, but the point of the calculation is to make yourself more effectively helpful. You, as teacher, are part of the situation, and although you look at it and see what it needs, you should also look at yourself and decide what you can give. Teachers who burn themselves out in a year may astound their colleagues and excite themselves, but they will not have been around long enough to have done the kids much good.

Such sour cynicism is a long way from most people's thoughts about teaching, and it was nowhere near mine when I started. I thought much more in personal terms, of the kind of person I would be in the class-room, and the image my pupils would have of me – intelligent, kind, perpetually interesting but still lovably human. Such fantasies feed voraciously on the inspiring autobiographies of heroic teachers, and are harmless enough in themselves, but of little relevance as a preparation for the job.

Such dreams deal largely with emotions; they have to, because before you start you cannot know what the realities are like. But emotions are controlled by situations more than the other way round, and a simple trust in good vibrations is a gamble if it depends for success on the same vibrations from thirty other individuals. The right feelings are important but not sufficient; some teachers who do not really like kids at all do a reasonable (in the circumstances, impressive) day's work, while others who love them find it impossible to teach at all.

Teaching is alive with emotional potential, but it also has its own technique and you are better off concentrating on that, at least until you have found your feet. Imagining classes fearing or loving you, admiring your talent or laughing at your jokes, is all very well, but children's emotions are even more fickle than those of adults, and make a doubtful foundation for what must be a working relationship. If you really like kids, that will show whatever you do and you will not need to demonstrate it deliberately; the same applies if you cannot stand them. If you are not sure, master the technique of the job, and that will give you some breathing space from which to judge whether you like it and the kids you teach. What I mean by 'technique' is elaborated in subsequent chapters, but it involves some of the cool rationality I have already proposed in discussing teacher-time. It also, in my view, involves some kind of impersonality (or, if that implies indifference, 'supra-personality'), in that the relationship between teacher and kids is not simply a meeting of persons. They are persons, but their meeting within the contexts of discipline is more than a personal relationship; when you tell children they must by law attend school and then group them into batches of thirty, you create relationships different from friendship, and though teachers and classes can and do become friends they rarely do so at once.

I am not arguing that all large groups are mindless, nor that compulsory schooling turns kids into monsters or vegetables – if you talk with actual kids, it obviously does not. They remain distinctive personalities, reacting in wholly different ways and capable of complex personal relationships with their teachers as well as with each other. In their previous schooling, however, before they met you, they encountered a wide range of teachers, who were aloof, friendly, sadistic, exciting, erratic, dull, reassuring or emotionally stifling. Because of this variety they cannot immediately be certain what kind of person you are, or what sort of relationship you offer, and it may be that you cannot be certain of that either. You therefore need to give them a gradual introduction to your personality by being initially impersonal.

Some may object that this is the thin end of a tyrant's wedge; the habit of dictatorship settles on both oppressor and oppressed, and you should start as you mean to go on. Impersonality, such critics might argue, denies the fullness of persons, de-personalises in fact, and this is the exact opposite of the teacher's proper function.

My reply is cautious and subjective. I can see the dangers, and concede that it is easy to become the prisoner of one's own routines. But the impersonality I propose is from the outset a temporary measure, deliberately though gradually disposable as soon as its purpose is achieved. For most kids in most schools today impersonality will not be a permanent blow, silencing them for good or stunting their growth; only ferocious sarcasm, vindictive injustice or irrational temper will make them 'switch off' with any finality. The reasons for such a measure are in my own case simply historical, in that my own first year in teaching began with a resolve to be personal and ended with me violent and depressed, erratic in my treatment of kids and of little use to them as either friend or teacher.

In *The Rainbow* D. H. Lawrence describes a similar process with sufficient conviction and power to provide a vivid example, of more universal relevance than my personal teaching history. Ursula Brangwen sets out to teach with high hopes and admirable objectives:

'She dreamed how she would make the little ugly children love her. She would be so *personal*. Teachers were always so hard and impersonal. There was no vivid relationship. She would make everything personal and vivid, she would give herself, she would give, give, give all her great stores of wealth to her children, she would make them *so* happy, and they would prefer her to any teacher on the face of the earth.'[1]

It is exactly this view of the 'personal' that is her downfall. She teaches a class of more than fifty kids from a rough part of Ilkeston. The buildings are drab, the staff repressive or resigned but uniformly unhelpful, and her class is literally too much for her:

'The children were her masters. She deferred to them. She could always hear Mr Brunt. Like a machine, always in the same hard, high inhuman voice he went on with his teaching, oblivious of everything. And before this inhuman number of children she was always at bay. She could not get away from it. There it was, this class of fifty collective children, depending on her for command, for command it hated and resented. It made her feel she could not breathe: she must suffocate, it was so inhuman. They were so beastly, that they were not children. They were a squadron. She could not speak as she would to a child, because they were not individual children, they were a collective, inhuman thing.'[2]

They are not of course, but that is how it feels. Ursula's reactions here exactly reflect the loathing of their situation, projected on to their pupils, felt by many young teachers when things go wrong. In Ursula's case, her depression and isolation are intensified by the rest of the staff. Mr Harby, the headmaster, comes in to watch her during her first week, but leaves without offering comment, criticism or consolation.

'The class was his class. She was a wavering substitute. He thrashed and bullied, he was hated. But he was master. Though she was gentle and always considerate of her class, yet they belonged to Mr Harby, and they did not belong to her. Like some invisible source of the mechanism he kept all power to himself. And the class owned his power. And in school it was power, and power alone that mattered.'[3]

[1] D. H. Lawrence, *The Rainbow* (Heinemann, 1915), p. 367.
[2] Ibid., pp. 376–7.
[3] Ibid., p. 377.

The rest of the staff are no more helpful. 'You have to keep order if you want to teach', she is told, and 'you have got to do it by yourself.'

Her headmaster despises her, her colleagues offer no help and her pupils do not simply disobey her but shout after her in the street. Finally, some of them throw stones at her and Ursula makes a ruthless, terrible decision:

'Never more, and never more would she give herself as an individual to her class. Never would she, Ursula Brangwen, the girl she was, the person she was, come into contact with those boys. She would be Standard Five teacher, as far away personally from her class as if she had never set foot in St Philip's School. She would just obliterate them all, and keep herself apart, take them as scholars only. . . . She, as teacher, must bring them all as scholars, into subjection. And this she was going to do. All else she would forsake. She had become hard and impersonal, almost avengeful on herself as well as on them, since the stone throwing. She did not want to be a person, to be herself any more, after such humiliation. She would assert herself for mastery, be only teacher. She was set now. She was going to fight and subdue.'[1]

She does fight, and she does subdue, but at terrible cost both to herself and to the children. This is, of course, only one example; a group of carefully selected extracts, from a novel written with great subjective involvement, cannot 'prove' anything. But they do follow with uncanny accuracy the course of many teaching apprenticeships: original high ideals, unrelated to the conditions of the job and ultimately selfish; the depressing impact of a staff-room, and sense of isolation within it by the misery of failure; the pressure of disapproval from an aloof headmaster, who suggests no specific solutions; and the extreme violence (both to pupils and to the teacher's own personality) of the swift change of policy, from generous, open love to tight assertion at all costs. I do not think I am unique in finding all these echoed in my own experience, nor in realising that the naïvety of my early view of the 'personal' contributed directly to the severity and injustice of the methods I later felt compelled to adopt.

I would argue that my own teaching has become more effective (by which I mean better for myself and the kids I teach), by the addition of a benevolent impersonality, which need not be anything like as stark and inhuman as Ursula's desperate change: 'She had become hard and impersonal. . . .' In fact, the earlier and more deliberately such an element is incorporated into one's teaching, the

[1] Ibid., pp. 395–6.

sooner is it possible to develop genuinely personal contacts, and to really get to know kids. There is, therefore, a double paradox: too 'personal' a start may well lead to inhuman severity later, whereas an 'impersonal' beginning may ultimately prove to be the best foundation for a close relationship between teacher and taught.

The impersonality is required, not as a corrective to juvenile crime, but as a consequence of mathematics: thirty children into one teacher does not go, and thirty children in a group are not any more capable of forming a 'personal relationship' with one adult than thirty adults would be with one child. Ursula Brangwen had difficulty, not because she was soft and the kids like sergeant-majors, but because she had too vague a picture of the kids she taught, and expected to simply transfer the values of a 1:1 relationship to 1:55.

Nowadays, in most class-rooms, there is one teacher, and about thirty pupils. He is paid and trained, while they are there by legal compulsion and need have no knowledge of or interest in his specialised field of knowledge. Teacher and taught will meet regularly over a year, after which they may or may not meet for another year. The times and places of their meetings will be arranged in advance, and quite independently of the parties involved, so that neither has the freedom to continue for an hour longer or to separate fifteen minutes earlier. None of these conditions apply to friendship, which is normally between individuals, equal in rank and acting of their own free will, meeting when they choose and only for so long as they desire.

In all these ways, the teacher is 'other'. He is also separate in the crucial sense that he alone is responsible for them all; no one else in the room is required to consider the needs of everyone in it, and although particular kids may well reveal astonishing awareness or consideration for others, only the teacher *must* think about them all. He alone must look beyond the present, both to record past progress and achievement, and to plan an interesting and relevant future. If he is at the mercy of his own emotional reactions, drawn by attraction and repelled by distaste, he will probably be unfair and certainly inefficient, failing those kids who are quiet, hostile, immature or dull. You do not have to love them all, but you do have to teach them, and that means building into your role some form of detachment, which will occasionally but regularly let you stand back from the excitement of personal contact and assess what is going on for each kid.

For young teachers starting work in a new and unfamiliar school, this is doubly important, since the temptations towards total immersion will be great, and the penalties for miscalculation severe. Not all probationers have as nasty an initiation as Ursula Brangwen, but some do, and often because they are too personal too soon. Kids, especially if they are insecure, need time to get to know someone; if it is to be a genuine relationship, it must be their choice as well as yours. A teacher who demands instant intimacy is failing his kids, by not trusting them to act for themselves, if and when they are ready. For all these reasons, but primarily for self-preservation, I think some kind of impersonality is essential.

This impersonality has nothing to do with formal etiquette, snobbish accents, hiding emotion or wearing charcoal suits. It is supremely practical: kids put up their hands when they wish to talk *because* there is no other way to ensure that they will be heard. The teacher should not entertain too extravagantly at first *because* kids not used to him will assume he will be like that for the rest of the year. Not exciting decisions, but cautious, negative injunctions which will not set the world alight but will do justice to the nature of the people present.

You may well be worried what this will do not merely to the kids but to yourself. Sadder and wiser men affirm that teaching warps the soul, and though after a mere six years I do not agree that this is necessarily true, it can be for some. 'In school it was power, and power alone that mattered' for Ursula Brangwen, and the exercise or pursuit of power affects some people almost as badly as its total loss. To advocate impersonality might seem to make things even worse, by encouraging probationers to suppress their most positive responses, precarious enough as they are. You look round at the wrinkled faces, padded elbows and fixed routines, and wonder what thirty more years of teaching might not do to you.

There cannot be a foolproof guarantee, beyond self-knowledge and common sense. It is harder the nicer you are, especially if it matters to you that people should like you; a limited insensitivity in this area can sometimes be a godsend. I do not think it is possible to teach effectively in a normal school and be liked all the time, but that does not mean I have enjoyed hearing comments like 'He never lets us do anything', 'Why do you always pick on me?' or 'Huh! worst teacher in school'. (This last a gem from my first year, at a school with a staff of eighty.) It seems unfair, when you have worked hard, meant well and attacked no one, to have resentment, boredom and contempt beamed powerfully in your direction; but occasional bursts of these are unavoidable. You accept them when you accept the job and the time-table and the responsibilities involved. If you absolutely refuse to impose your will over anyone else's, and cannot bear not to be liked all the time, you will either have to do private tuition or be very careful how you pick your school.

If, on the other hand, you accept the risks and compromises, it is rapidly worthwhile; even my first year, with blunders, depressions and occasional riots, also had its positive excitements. And as you get better, and the kids get used to you and working with you, so your discipline problems diminish and your freedom to be yourself grows. With confidence, established through experience and occasionally being a swine, you relax; you learn what to tolerate and what to prevent, and create a secure space in which both you and your kids can learn and be human. It takes time, but it does happen.

It does not all fall into place in a week, though, and there will always be times when you are sick of the pettiness, strife or thankless grind of the whole operation. It is then that you comfort yourself by reflecting that teaching, though a privilege and a pleasure, a vocation and a sacrament, is also a job, and in that there is some sanity.

Chapter 6

Kids in Classes

Kids in General

Kids are people and so – less often remembered – are teachers, but their encounters are not simply personal meetings. In schools, within the contexts of discipline, we group kids into batches of thirty, and call them classes. But though they may come to you as 4E1 or 2C, at 4 o'clock they go home as Pete, Susan and Marion. The teacher therefore needs to resist the temptation to 'mass' kids in his mind. He may not be able to respond sensitively to each individual in every class, but that should lead to a humble admission of ignorance rather than to rapid conclusions about 'the quality of 4E1', 'the behaviour of 2C' or, even worse, a universal notion of 'what kids are like'.

Such general views stem more often from the feelings and wishes of their holders than from close observation of particular children. Many teachers, for instance, will assure you with total confidence that 'kids like to know who is boss', and then go on to use that as a justification for irrational and destructive control. Kids do not enjoy the uncertainty of a class-room riot, and they do like to know 'where they stand' with a teacher – in other words, what is likely to happen, what they will be asked to do and what will happen if they do not co-operate. But this is a specific need for clarity, not a general demand for slave status. Certainly, kids like to be set work clearly, and to be asked questions which make sense to them, but I have found very little evidence that they want to be told how to run their friendships or their sex lives; nor do many of them want to be told which beliefs to hold or which clothes to wear. (They may well consult sympathetic adults on all these matters, but only because they have chosen to do so.) Yet there are still some school régimes which defend their pettiest, most oppressive and least necessary regulations on the vague ground that 'children like a firm framework of order'.

The psychological truth, therefore, that children are unhappy under a serious crisis of authority, and need some kind of certainty, should not be erected into an absolute faith in imposition. Some imposition may be necessary, and some teachers will want to overrule the immediate wishes and choices of their pupils, but that should be a

rational decision, openly justified if possible, and certainly not supported by a blanket assertion about universal characteristics and
needs.

For any teacher of any awareness, constant contact with kids will
in any case continually alter any view ever held about 'what kids are
like'. I can remember the feeling of shock which hit me when I
discovered that the vast majority of third year boys in the toughest
class I have ever taught ran off to ATC after school. They spent a large
part of their day disputing with authority, questioning orders and
refusing to wear uniform, and as soon as their time was their own
they made a bee-line for an organisation which told them what to
wear, made them obey every order without explanation and marched
them around for no obvious purpose. This, apart from undermining
my democratic assumptions about kids wanting independence, did not
seem to relate at all to the school behaviour of those boys; even if
I had wanted, I could not have moved simply to the opposite extreme
faith and concluded that 'kids want firm authority', since on those
occasions when the school provided it they were just as rebellious and
resistant as they were to most other teachers. I was forced, therefore,
to refine my simple view, so as to take account of various kids and
various forms of authority; the same kids, experience showed me,
might reject the (childish?) authority of school and accept the less
rational (but more adult?) authority of ATC.

The wants, and needs, of children in terms of discipline are obviously
various, and the existing complexity of individual variations in character is further complicated by the factors of age and sex. We justify
many of our actions by the simple fact that the children we teach
are younger than we are, but rarely do we work out the full implications of this. We say 'children are too young to decide for themselves,
so we shall act in their best interests', without working out precisely
how young they are, or how old they need to be before becoming
capable of taking that particular decision. It may not be possible to
produce a neat scale of which freedoms should be allowed at which
ages, and it is obviously true that some 13-year-old girls are more
mature than some 15-year-old boys, but this still does not mean that
all pupils should be treated in the same way.

A rationally graded allowance of freedom, however, is in the future,
and of little immediate comfort to the young teacher trying to find a
realistic view of kids which will enable him to teach effectively. I
would suggest he limit himself to two generalisations, both of which
derive from the age of his clients and both of which should govern
his own behaviour:

G

(1) Most kids, whatever façade they present, are more vulnerable than most adults, simply because their indentities are more obviously in the process of formation, and therefore more open to attack.

(2) Nearly all kids, confronted with a new teacher, need to explore as fully as possible his personality and competence.

The significance of the kid's vulnerability for the teacher is that he should avoid it. There are desperate times of crisis, in which nothing seems more important than trying to break the kid who threatens to break you, when any weapon at all will do – insults, sarcasm, humiliation or physical assault. Even at those times, however, I would urge the counsel of perfection, and try to avoid direct attack on the person the kid is. 'You are a right little bastard, Armitage, and I'm sick of you', tells Armitage what you think of him, but is unlikely to change him. Next day, when you have got over it and wish you had not said it, he will not have forgotten, and though he may be sulky, aggressive or subdued it will be very difficult to make positive contact. Within secure relationships, of course, all kinds of mutual threat and diabolic insult are possible, but they take time and care to construct.

In the lower pressure of day-to-day teaching I would try to keep attention off personalities wherever possible, and objectify my comments by continually relating them to the work. To the teacher, this may seem a transparent device, but to many kids it offers a helpful layer of defence. So, 'This ends a bit quick, doesn't it?' or 'What's your group going to do, then?' are less offensive than 'You idle child, this story is far too short' or 'What are you layabouts up to?' There is less chance of an abusive or sullen reply, and therefore more likelihood of a positive response.

Such delicate restraint feels very unfair when you are confronted with kids to whom nothing is sacred. Some children at war with a teacher will use anything they can lay their hands or tongues on – clothes, voice, family, hair, love life, walk, mannerisms or supposed lack of sexual attraction. It seems an uneven battle to take on enemies so formidably equipped, when the accepted teacher's weapons are politeness, rational argument, persuasion and a formal array of inappropriate sanctions – but that is part of the job. Retaliating in kind, although natural and at moments irresistible, almost always causes more trouble than it solves.

The second general characteristic of kids in classes involves what I call 'sniffing out'. Each class by necessity explores the potential of a newcomer by activity designed to establish his or her limits – whether of vision, patience, strength, intelligence, embarrassment or fear. This process may not be as drastic as it was for Ursula Brangwen (although it certainly can be) but it does seem widely necessary. Any average class, given basic liveliness and the absence of a frightening régime, will present to its teacher not only a collection of separate, fascinating individual lives, but also a composite and demanding questionnaire, to be unwittingly completed in its presence. During this instinctive examination the class will discover most of the aspects of that teacher which will have disciplinary relevance.

This may not be immediately apparent. Many innocent probationers have walked home after the first day of the school year quietly smiling ('they are not that bad, really'), only to be hit by an avalanche three weeks later. But those three weeks have been carefully spent, by the class if not by the teacher, and by the end of that time the kids will know what will earn praise and blame, where they can go, what they can do and say, and at which point undesirable retribution will begin. Such calculations are not usually consciously planned or communally arranged, and may well take place in an atmosphere of mutual attraction between teacher and taught but, like a dog entering a strange room, they have to have a good sniff first.

The means of sniffing are endless. Firstly, physical: limbs, shifting of position, taking off jackets and ties, changing furniture round, closing blinds, opening windows, fetching board dusters, dropping desk lids, shunting chairs, leaning back on them and – well, well, well, it has fallen over. 'I didn't mean it, sir', and the sly comedian grins in apology and triumph as he gets his first public laugh (of many?) in your helpless presence. There are times when the conventional academic equipment seems like a torturer's delight: pens, paper, ruler, compasses and a rubber. Just try to think of five objects with more diabolic potential: prodding, dropping, tapping, flying aeroplanes, passing notes, smearing ink, creating rubbish, twanging, assaulting others, carving desks, throwing, rolling, bouncing and swallowing. Every one of them *might* be innocent, and any one in the wrong hands will be sufficient to waste hours of preparation and deprive your lesson of its original sense of structure.

And all that assumes thirty kids acting as individuals, dumbly. Just add the tangles of teenage relationship and the power of the adolescent mouth and your fate is sealed. Arguments between friends, bullying, emotional crises, accidents with other kids' bags or coats, theft and the endless search for a friendly philanthropist – 'Can I try and borrow a pen, miss?' – are all entertainments in their own right, but also peculiarly common in the first weeks of September. How common they become after that is decided, one way or the other, by the teacher.

Most of this sniffing out will not be conscious, and much of the worst of it is quite irrational. Light humming from different parts of the room, a volley of accidentally dropped pencils, an ear-piercing whistle when every mouth seems closed, or a stream of inadequate bladders do not seem to serve any useful purpose. The teacher may well find them alien, and privately despise them; he can, if he wants, despise them publicly, but that will not help. What he must do is find some way to act which retains the initiative and leaves him free to move.

Quite how you should act, and react, in these crucial first few weeks is outlined in the suggestions of the two chapters which follow. It is a difficult series of problems, because each situation is slightly different, and each teacher is variously equipped, so that other people's solutions may well not seem appropriate. What is important at this stage, however, in considering kids in classes, is simply to recognise that most classes will need some form of 'sniffing out' before they can trust or work usefully with a new teacher. How prolonged, open or malicious this is will depend on them and on him, but it will almost inevitably take place.

Age and Sex: Some Generalisations

Any one teacher sees only a glimpse of his pupils' total lives, and only a small fraction of the pupil world within school. Much of the important traffic (in ideas, gossip, friendships and crime) takes place safely out of teacher's vision, and staff-room generalisations should therefore be delivered with extreme caution. There is no guarantee that pupils appear to each other as they do to us, and there are certain but subtle boundaries drawn by intelligence, will power, social groupings, contacts outside school, criminal experience, physical strength or attraction and so on, of which teachers may not always be aware, but which to pupils may well be decisive influences upon their behaviour. Individuals or groups who may seem popular, friendly or mature to a teacher may be quite differently viewed by their peers, and we can therefore be confident neither in our dealings with the pupil world nor in our pronouncements upon it. Nonetheless, the wary probationary teacher is entitled to some general guidelines on pupil behaviour as it may affect his classes, and it is for this purpose that the following notes are offered.

YEARS 1 AND 2 Often the kids are genuinely excited by their new school, especially if it is big and full of unfamiliar but promising facilities. Some first-year pupils go round in a constant blaze of excitement, finding everything very interesting and worthy of comment. The early problems are therefore not so much to do with fighting crooks as with establishing routines and procedures through which to channel this enthusiasm. Shouting all at once is a common pastime, and fidgeting, calling out and quarrelling over trifles should also be expected. Every experience is felt to be intensely important, so a beautifully organised lesson may well be interrupted by an entirely irrelevant 'I can't find my pencil.' Hysterical rows over who sits where, who has stolen Jane's pen (safely in her bag) or the exact nature of last night's homework, are also commonplace and very tiring; few first-year kids will seem totally evil but a lot can be very exhausting.

With their second year in school some of this excitement will wear off, though at different rates for different kids. Playing up teacher will come to seem more attractive, and the combined experiences of growing older, having first years below them and knowing their way around school will all contribute to a greater sense of maturity though the painful incompleteness of that maturity will also make for more sourness and fewer open confessions and anecdotes than were offered the previous year. The majority of girls will be concerned with their intimate friendships, whereas the boys will be louder, messier and keener to challenge authority – especially if it resembles the mum they think they are growing out of at home.

YEARS 3, 4 AND 5 The 'difficult' years, and certainly the source of most teachers' discipline problems. The 'big new school' excitement will probably have evaporated completely, and so in many cases will the enthusiasm for work. Teachers are no longer the freshly promising adults they appeared to be two years ago, and the work is familiar enough to be dull, without being really advanced enough to be demanding or for a large minority, useful. Those who are not any good at work will by now feel that it is not worth trying, as they are not going to get any better; it will be easier, and probably more fun, to muck about instead. School may not be an important part of life, and will often be seen as repressive, stopping them from doing what they want in the evenings, not letting them wear what they want during the day, and so on. Teachers are a good target on which to practise growing maturity, whether it be through a stand-up row or subtle fluttering of eyelashes. Peer group friendships will be important but also fragile, and a lot of kids at this age will feel lonely or insecure, although they often will not want to admit that to a teacher.

As they get older the sheer silliness will get less; quite a few kids I have known who were devils lower down the school have in fact improved in the fourth year, against staff expectations. If there is real bitterness, however, it will have grown deeper, and all the more so for ROSLA postponing hopes of possible release. Those who have made a habit of playing up will by now have a polished repertoire and a long experience of various punishments; however confused or vulnerable within, it will also have become part of their role to show no sign of interest, repentance or mercy. Even normal kids, well-disposed towards school, may occasionally welcome the variety of mucking about, and will certainly resent being treated like the little children they were two years ago – whether by selection of work, petty regulations or the tone of the teacher's voice.

SIXTH YEARS   You would not expect these years to provide a discipline problem, and for precisely that reason it is worth taking care. There will be less silliness (although there will be some, just as there is with teachers) and fewer outright confrontations, but there may well be serious tension over restrictions on freedom. The past models of sixth-form behaviour generally have been based on a pattern of school-leaving which is rapidly changing. We are increasingly going to be faced with youngsters of 16 and 17 who are not especially clever, not committed to the school régime by the hopes of their parents or the prospect of a university place, and the problems thus set for teachers could be considerable.

   In my own teaching, I find it so great a relief from the pressure of petty regulation lower down the school that I tend to over-react with sixth-formers, involving them in lively and open discussion very readily but not always keeping quite so close an eye upon rates and quality of work as I might. This is a subtle form of discipline problem, with clear dangers at the other extreme as well, but it does bear thinking about.

GIRLS   They tend to have more powerful feelings (or to suppress them less?), and thus tend to continue feuds with both peers and staff longer and more intensely. A girl wounded by sarcasm or made to look ridiculous will take a lot longer to forgive the teacher responsible than a boy would; sometimes the most casual friendly crack will be taken to heart for a whole term, so be safe rather than sorry. Girls care more for appearance than boys, as their obsession with their hair and clothes suggests, and are thus more susceptible to appeals to the look of a piece of work. Their fear of humiliation, love of neatness and acceptance, and involvement in their passionate friendships all tend to keep them out of trouble more than the boys.

There are, however, exceptions, and a girl who does not care what anyone elses sees, hears or thinks is the most frightening proposition in teaching – at least to a man! Girls of 13–16 can be much more worldly than boys; they consequently see through teacher-bluffs more perceptively and must not be allowed to make you lose your temper. Conversely, they can sometimes be gently kidded out of potential hostility by a careful relaxation of pressure.

(With men teachers) Younger girls will often respond to the 'games with daddy' approach, or alternatively be quite blindly attracted by superficial appearance. This is flattering, but can be followed by bitter disillusionment if teaching performance does not live up to visual promise. As girls get older they naturally find men teachers convenient dummies on which to try out their feminine charms, which may feel complimentary but obviously needs watching. If the claims of morality or discretion do not appeal, think of the disciplinary consequences of a lively group of fifth-year boys finding out that you are going out with one of their classmates.

(With women teachers) There are times when girls like to have sexual allies on the staff, but they can also be fiercer than the boys in attacking women teachers. The roots of nastiness go deeper, and for less cause; unattractive appearance, snobbish voice, clothes of a different style can each trigger off a totally irrational dislike which is most unnerving for the victim.

BOYS They are generally louder, messier and more open. They can be very silly, but are usually less devious and therefore easier both to detect and to punish. Talking to girls gives you much less idea of how much is going in; boys tend either to look sullen, cry, show obvious boredom or fake a repentance which is so transparent that it makes you laugh.

As they grow older their assumption of masculinity becomes both important and precarious; in really tight situations you may want to expose this and remind them that they are still little boys, but this can be cruel and dangerous. Where possible, allow time for a dignified defeat, which leaves you in charge without directly humiliating them (e.g. 'Clear that mess up by the end of the lesson' or 'Make sure you are out of here by the time I come back', rather than actually standing over them, demanding public submission).

On the positive side, there is a real keenness to be active, which not only can result in errands saving your legs, but also can incorporate difficult boys into the course of a lesson; fetching a tape-recorder, putting on a record, even wiping the blackboard, can for *some* boys provide a useful semi-adult role. To others, of course, it will be crawling.

(With men teachers) Those boys who most like rigid discipline are more likely to get it from men, and some will reject any attempt at it from a woman, however competent. Really tough boys, too, may grow intensely attached to a particular teacher, doing jobs for him while treating the rest of the staff with indifference or contempt. This kind of tie is not predictable or transferable, but it is worth knowing that it can happen. Among younger boys, silliness can be quickly quelled by a firm shout or appearance of physical strength, but as an aid to discipline the latter is generally overrated.

(With women teachers) There are a few boys who really ought to be taught by men, but these are a small number of special cases. A lot of women teachers are far more successful than cynics would expect in dealing with even the roughest lads. Their techniques vary, and some of them exceed mere male understanding, but among their qualities is coolness; not in the sense of indifference but in their maintenance of poise, whether telling off 6-foot boys or being chatted up by a group of adolescent admirers; the anger or affection is genuine, but in each case something is held back, miss remains in charge of herself and therefore of her class-room. Weakness may well provoke private sympathy, but few lads will expose themselves by protecting a woman teacher in class, so appeals for pity will produce little response.

With younger boys, even quite young women work wonders with a skilful motherliness, backed up by painstaking preparation and marking, plus a careful attention to detail. This may involve some nagging, which is unpleasant, resented and unattractive, but can be effective. Whining and shrieking, by contrast, are not.

The resemblance to mum may be a real handicap higher up the age range but the obvious alternative role (miss as fairy princess) calls for a chilling self-control that few can manage. Women teachers, however, worry less about their image than about their efficiency, usually find that as they acquire competence and confidence, so their boy pupils take less pleasure in trying to torment them, and they demand far less from their nerves and vocal chords.

These comments are teacher-centred and gloomy, as befits a book about discipline. The picture is bound to be negative, since the kids who are interested in their work and do as you ask will present no discipline problem; this catalogue, therefore, is offered merely as a collection of specific warnings, rather than as a fully sensitive portrait of pupil behaviour in school.

Classes, Groups and Individuals

The teacher encounters his pupils as a class, as groups and as individuals. Although a full picture of class activity would have to deal with all three simultaneously, the apprehensive teacher is best off keeping within human limits and progressing one step at a time; first deal with a class, then become aware of its separate groups and finally become involved with individuals. Many individuals will not allow so orderly a progression, demanding special attention within minutes of the term's first lesson, but I would still suggest class – groups – individuals as the ideal sequence.

The alternative, concentrating immediately on those in apparent need, seems perfectly plausible and attractively romantic – plodding off over the fields after the one while the ninety and nine chew happily unattended. But adolescents are not sheep, and need rather more attention, information and stimulus, all of which it is the job of the teacher to provide. Spending all your time on the problems of one child may well feel nice, but if it is done too soon it will leave the rest of the class bitterly wondering why they are not worthy of such dedication; the more logical may even invent tantrums to place themselves among the privileged few upon whom the teacher expends real effort. Individual help is of course vital, and should be a part of each class teacher's repertoire, but only within a context of overall purpose which is also part of the job. Thinking in terms of the class as a whole, of what they need to do and which conditions will help them best, should create a pattern of work which will in time allow the teacher to spend disproportionate lesson-time on individual problems; but if that concentration is too early or too blatant the whole enterprise breaks down. Kids not spoken to become restless, either disrupting to gain attention, or listlessly sulking to no purpose; some of them may watch the teacher's efforts with the lucky individual, so distorting the 1:1 relationship and putting even further strain on the teacher.

You deal, then, with the class, and the first thing you need to remember is that it is not a thirty-piece entity, dropped from the skies, but the deliberate creation of the school time-table. Some classes have a strong corporate identity, some are made up of fragmented groups continually at war with each other, and others change character dramatically during the course of a teaching year. If they are streamed they will know it, whatever clumsy devices the school may have chosen to hide Plato's traditional divisions of Gold, Silver and Bronze. With bottom-stream groups, who quite reasonably provide more discipline problems than their more favoured peers, it is not worth referring to their status at all. 'I heard you lot were bad, but this is ridiculous' will obviously be counter-productive, but 'I don't care what they call you, I think you are the best class in school' will not be much better. Kids in bottom streams have been told they are useless for a large part of their school life, and will need more than a verbal reassurance in the first week of term for things to really change. What you say, therefore, is of secondary importance; what you do, and how you treat them over the year, are the things that really matter.

This is a good argument against listening to anything about the kids you teach from other teachers, but I would not make that a total rule. Some hints can be most useful in preparing you for what to expect from individuals, and sometimes the background history of a whole form can be crucial. How have they been streamed or set, and for how long? Is there any recent event which might be relevant – significant new arrivals, friendships broken up, promotions or demotions? Which teacher did they have for this particular subject, and how did he get on with them? Is there a form teacher or tutor who could supply useful information on family backgrounds? Are house or department records of past progress available?

For considering actual class management, I would suggest seeing them as a spectrum, representing the class as follows:

```
x x x x x x x x x x x x x x x
                                          O
x x x x x x x x x x x x x x x
CROOKS        MIDDLE OF THE ROAD      ANGELS        TEACHER
```

Many crooks do prefer to operate from the back row, but this should not be taken as a seating diagram. All it describes are the different degrees of trouble you may need to anticipate; at one extreme the fearless hard case, at the other the saint who goes on with her work even when curses, desks and pencils are falling like morning rain. Character is not simply static, and between those extremes many variations are possible: some kids will be angels in some lessons and crooks in others, and many will have a week when they suddenly go out of character and speed to the opposite end of the spectrum. The teacher, too, will help determine who does what; a calm, experienced member of staff may make a gang of bottom stream crooks appear angelic, while a disorganised beginner can turn almost any kid into a trouble-maker through sheer frustration.

Given such a spectrum, the teacher's initial task is to establish a 'line of control', if possible to include the whole class, but at any rate as far to the left as possible. The control is temporary and superficial (outlined in detail in the following chapter) but still necessary, and the whole class-view is essential for its effective operation. The line is defined through looks, comments and ultimately sanctions, the aim of which is to deter both that individual crook and others from a repeat performance. If the line can be held far to the left, it will exclude only the inveterate crooks:

```
X   X  ║  X  X  X  X  X  X  X  X  X  X  X  X  X
        ║                                              O
X   X  ║  X  X  X  X  X  X  X  X  X  X  X  X  X
CROOKS  ║      MIDDLE OF THE ROAD      ANGELS        TEACHER
```

If the teacher has concentrated on establishing that line, and achieving the conditions which will enable the majority of kids to work, he has more of a chance to cope with unforeseen crises. If the rest of the class are genuinely busy – and not simply dulled by a temporary threat – he can talk to one kid outside the room, without the distraction of an audience. The control line thus offers a short-term aim, crude but practical, and a useful tool between the extremes of order and chaos, that middle ground of compromise where the pro-bationer teacher learns his trade. The question he should ask is not 'Do they do what I say?' but 'How many of them do what I say?'; more complete control, and more impressive teaching, is eventually possible, but the definition of this line is the easiest and simplest preliminary to it.

If there is no overall class strategy, but simply an instinctive im-provisation to whatever happens, the diagram looks like this:

```
X  X  X  X  X  X  X  X  X  X  X  X  ║  X  X  X
                                     ║                 O
X  X  X  X  X  X  X  X  X  X  X  X  ║  X  X  X
CROOKS      MIDDLE OF THE ROAD        ║  ANGELS      TEACHER
```

The crooks who first dared to cross the traditional lines (moving from desks, yelling out, interrupting the teacher) have proved to the others that it can be done, and the incentive to explore further is there. The teacher may have issued occasional threats or punishments, but unless these have been clear and consistent they will not provide a reason for the crooks to stop. The middle-of-the-road kids, who might originally have gone either way, will have joined in, since they have little choice. If others can fight, move around and ignore the work they should be doing, why should they insist on working? The absence of control gives them little incentive, and there is a powerful deterrent in the contempt the hard core will show to anyone who is working when he does not have to. Most kids do not want a total riot, but nearly all of them will join in when anarchy starts, simply because there does not seem to be another role offering comparable safety. Nor is the situation static; the urge to explore means that mucking about does not remain on a steady level, as it might if it were a simply rational pastime. It escalates alarmingly. If you can pass a note, flick a pencil or kick the girl in front of you, why not eat crisps, throw a dart or stick a pin in her backside? By the end, only the most determined angels will still be on the side of the law, and they are the most powerful rebuke of all, since their puritanical outrage shrilly underlines the teacher's loss of control but continuing responsibility.

Some teachers argue that they do not want 'control'. The word smacks of domination, and they are right to fear its effect on both ruler and ruled. But concern for one's own personality and a distaste for self-assertion do not justify the teacher's abdication from an authoritative role; for the consequence of anarchy is not merely that kids 'do what they like'. Some of them do what they like, briefly, but even if the riot becomes boring or wearing they are effectively powerless to stop it. Once the framework of control (to which their previous school career has largely accustomed them) has been broken, they cannot simply restore it by an act of will, and in the process of breakdown a large number of kids go through painful uncertainties and fears. Some uncertainties and fears may be useful, even necessary, but no one who has witnessed a riot which was his responsibility would seriously claim that it was for the kids a valuable learning experience. That responsibility remains with the teacher, and is increased rather than diminished the further the class moves out of his control.

If the teacher can establish a 'line of control', he immediately makes future prospects for himself and the kids much brighter. As they become used to you, the pressure is taken off both sides, and with intelligent observation and accurate recording you build up an awareness of the different groups within one class. Within the order you have created you will be able to talk intensively with one particular group, or send another out to act, film or tape-record. Also, you will have time in which to adjust hurried first impressions; a group of large, noisy boys may turn out to be entirely benevolent, and the attractive pair of girls who seemed eager to impress may in fact be difficult and moody. Eventually, you can use natural groupings as a positive force, confidently creating working groups because you know the patterns which will most fully involve their members, and incidentally take some of the performing strain off you. Treating kids as groups is a complex skill to which sociograms are only a partial aid, and you need to allow constantly for the shifting movement of alliances which will take place in any form during the course of a school year. Simply labelling apparent groups at the beginning of the year – 'you lot', 'that table', 'the thickies on the back row' – will probably insult them and certainly blind you to the serious differences between the individuals they contain.

Ultimately, and rightly, you deal with individuals. In the long run the committed teacher must be concerned with each of the people he claims to teach, and not simply with those who interest, attract, amuse or disturb him. But this detailed knowledge is the work of a lifetime, developed with sensitivity and skill by the best teachers and certainly not mastered within a few months. The young teacher, at the beginning of a new school year as well as of his own career, must search for an overall strategy which will involve his class as a whole, and only when that has been successfully pursued will he be free to concentrate on the more important, hazardous and rewarding business of individual relationships.

Problem Kids

Into this smooth rhythm of increasingly individual attention, a number of characters may well insert themselves very forcefully, demanding immediate response from the teacher. In any large school with reasonably varied intake there will be a small group who present the staff as a whole with problems quite disproportionate to their numbers. Whether this problematical élite are in fact a separate group, or simply the extreme end of the discipline spectrum, does not greatly matter; the pressing fact is that they present most staff with a real difficulty in that they cannot be contained within the limits of a conventional class-room, and often cannot be contained within legitimate society when they leave school.

Ideally, young teachers will not be confronted with such extreme cases in their first year of teaching, or at least will not be asked to teach them in isolation from other members of staff. Many schools, however, are not ideal, and though the pernicious tradition of 'easiest classes to most experienced staff' is belatedly dying, it is by no means unheard of for a probationer teacher to take on a bottom stream, third or fourth year group, with no guidance or support from other staff. In any case, no teacher in a large comprehensive can hope to avoid particular types of kids for very long; dinner duties, substituting for absent colleagues and simply walking along corridors will in time ensure that most teachers meet most types of pupil.

For most seriously difficult kids there are powerful factors at work outside school, pressuring the kid into anti-social behaviour. This is not to say that all trouble-makers are innocent, nor does it deny that many kids triumphantly overcome broken homes, regular cruelty and real squalor; it does suggest, however, that very few of the kids who make war on a whole school are reacting rationally to the situation, by deliberate and happy choice. Most of the really difficult kids I have known were essentially lonely and frustrated, and not really fulfilled by their rebellion, although it may well have seemed to them the best of a grim set of alternatives. For the teacher, this means that he may bear no responsibility for the hostility which he encounters; that does not mean he has to ignore it, nor that he should enjoy being sworn at or defied, but it does reaffirm the obvious truth that these kids bring into school and their school behaviour a whole battery of pressures unknown to the teacher and beyond his control.

There are still ways, however, of making such meetings better or worse. Immediate offers of friendship, like booming threats, are no help at all: such a kid has explored the resources of adult vocabulary very thoroughly, and been sworn at, coaxed, pleaded with, prayed over and condemned. He has seen friendly façades crack before, and of each teacher he wants to know, not what they will say to impress, but how in a crisis they will treat him. Like southpaws in boxing, the difficult kid has met the normal teacher more often than the normal teacher has met him, so a well-intentioned probationer had better step very warily before presuming to solve a problem which probably goes back for years.

In the pressures of the teaching situation, you normally have time only to seek the most precarious, short-term solutions. With a really disturbed kid you can have no guarantee that after two weeks of peaceful coexistence he will not get up, throw a book at another pupil, pour ink over someone else's work, swear at the teacher and walk out. If, on the other hand, you are jumpy and suspicious, and unwittingly communicate that you are expecting him to erupt, you will accelerate the trouble for which you are preparing. The only self-defence I would offer is that where possible confrontations should be kept on a 1:1 basis, and that when it comes to a crunch decision you should choose the rest of the class rather than any individual kid. This may mean calling in other members of staff, which is embarrassing at the best of times, but that is preferable to sending him off to the educational sin-bin of the library or trying doggedly to solve the insoluble within the walls of a class-room which increasingly become too small and too thin.

In confrontation, you always have more to lose. A really disturbed kid has nothing to fear, because he may well have already survived worse fates than you could even contemplate. You, on the other hand, intend to carry on teaching the rest of the class and for that reason (rather than for considerations of self-esteem) you do not want to appear too ridiculous. A second-year boy, who was lifted up in anger by a teacher, looked round the class coolly and said 'It's nice up here', gaining a general laugh and totally deflating the teacher; what could you do after that except put him down and admit defeat? In public, with a watching class, you are always more vulnerable and for that reason you need to avoid confrontations rather than to win them.

Some teachers in lucky moments do find exactly the right comment or action to deflate a difficult kid, like going down on their knees and pleading for mercy, or pretending to be in love with a troublesome girl, but this needs a lot of nerve and experience; if it misfires you are worse off than you were before. In caution, then, I would recommend keeping out of competition; do not try to be stronger than the little lad who is fighting, wittier than the practical joker, more sarcastic than the girl in the corner or more obscene than the connoisseur of filth. Even if you win that particular contest, you are inviting further challenges by implying that class-room supremacy goes to the toughest, wittiest, nastiest or dirtiest, and even if all those labels fit you it will be hard work to keep having to prove it.

In crisis, say the minimum. If the kid is prepared to defy you he will not be dissuaded simply by logic or eloquence, but he might be slowed down by calm. The more hostile words you give him the more he will have to chew on – violent disagreement, angry questions or crippling, lethal politeness: 'Sorry, sir? . . . You what? . . . Who, me?' and so on, punctuating your tirade so regularly that you forget what you wanted to say.

Only experience sorts out the compulsively disturbed child from the mucker-about trying it on, but in either case patience and calm work best, since they commit you least. If you are calm you might still become angry, but once you are angry you will find it hard to go back. With a kid under strong internal pressure, it takes only the slightest external pressure for him to be away, out of his own and your control, and probably anybody else's. Threats, insults or physical contact will only make things worse, and so will sustained teacher pressure – 'When you get on to me, I just can't help myself', as a self-aware problem once told me. Take away the pressure of teacher and the class, the demands for obedience and action, and such a kid's life may become manageable again, but within that class-room no teacher, least of all a new one, can hope to achieve that miracle.

To such problems (and they are a tiny proportion of the school population) the answers will not come from you alone. Other teachers may well seem to have a strange power over a child you personally find unmanageable, but that is not because they have learned particular tricks or appropriate threats. It is much more likely that they have got to know the kid in question and have taught him for at least a year, so that they are at least partially accepted. This process cannot be hurried, and you just have to accept that there are severe limits on what you can achieve with some adolescent pupils, because there is not enough time to get to know them before they leave. This is frustrating for you and a loss for them, but you have the vague consolation of knowing that if you stay for three years you will do better with your fourth years by the time you leave.

The final point about problem kids is that, quite unwittingly, they help the teacher. The prospect of chaos, like that of execution, concentrates the mind wonderfully, and a difficult kid who may tear your room apart at the first sign of boredom can be an effective deterrent to sloppy planning or mechanical syllabi. Often you are forced into rigorous thinking which would simply not take place if all pupils were obedient, law-abiding and polite. At the moment, too, when I hover on the edge of heartbreak, desperate to find a lever which will break some child before he or she breaks me, it does me no harm to remember that I would not really want a control panel in my desk to manipulate every child; on a bad day it would save my nerves, but in the long run it would make for boredom and a terrifying responsibility. When the class is full of robots no one ever has any trouble, but you do not get any life or learning either, and the teacher at the controls is irrevocably alone. So the really hard case, tragic in himself and irritating in the short term, can act as a necessary reminder that we do not deal with puppets, we do not seek the status of gods, we are not in total control.

Chapter 7

Survival

The teacher's first duty is to survive. That may sound melodramatic – but only to those who have survived without effort or to those who have never needed to try. Teachers aware of the pressures on their younger colleagues would not dismiss survival as a fanciful initial aim; they would see it rather as the essential precondition of real growth, for teachers and pupils alike.

In this chapter I try to indicate in precise detail how this survival can best be achieved. Such advice will necessarily be subjective, drawing heavily on my own experiences and problems, which may well not be identical with those of other teachers. To competent teachers or well-trained students, much of what follows may seem obvious; to those experienced in really difficult schools it will be laughably inadequate; to some young teachers, however, it may be a useful outline, both as an indication of some unforeseen snags and also as a specific example against which to react. A reading of this chapter may well provoke violent disagreement and contrary suggestion, but that very response will be fruitful, in further refining a complicated discussion, which is currently carried out in the vaguest possible terms.

What I offer is at least specific, encapsulating the hard-won wisdom I wish I had had six years ago. It will not fit all teachers, all kids or all situations, but it may well encourage a wider sharing of experience and insight, and it is at least a start. Each night a horde of lonely teachers slink home to miserable preparation and the private conviction of failure, and we owe them some form of assistance more concrete than comforting platitudes.

Plan of Action

For the purposes of this outline, I assume that you are teaching a third-year bottom-stream class, and that you have been left to decide material and procedures for yourself. This is neither a universal nor an ideal situation, but it is common; if you happen to have a perfect syllabus, enlightened school régime or helpful head of department, count your blessings.

H

The first time you meet the class you should try to ensure that the room is as you want it, and that the pupils wait outside until you are ready for them to come in. If they burst in, out of malice or through genuine misunderstanding, politely but firmly ask them to go outside and wait. It is probably easier if they wait in two lines so as to leave general thoroughfares free, but you must decide what you want before they come in and try to ensure that they keep to it. From the first moment they meet you you must seek to suggest control of the situation, not by adopting a Napoleonic stance or an artificial tone, but simply by taking the important decisions. What you do is more important than what you say you will do, so do not preach, cajole or threaten – just get on with it.

Let them into the room, having explained where you want them to sit. I personally let kids sit where they want, but have known hardened trouble-shooters to seat a class alphabetically. Do not at this stage allow kids to start moving furniture or squabbling over who sits where. If there is any doubt, you must decide quickly, and keep to it; at this early stage you have the initiative – for all they know you might be a brilliant teacher, so do not disillusion them. If you want to have a clear, formal start to the lesson, ask the kids to go into the room and then stand up when you come in; it is petty, but it does ritualise your central role. I do not do it myself, but know excellent teachers who do, and who think it helps. Either way, if anyone comes late after you have begun, do not ignore it. If the course of the lesson is so vitally interesting that you do not want to interrupt it, simply make a note of the name and time of the late arrival and see him or her at the end of the lesson; but establish, as early as you can, that you care about starting on time and that you will want to know in full the alibis of late arrivals.

Assuming that everyone is in place and on time, your first job is to know who is who, partly because you cannot effectively teach kids you do not know, but also because as a discipline precaution you will need to know names as soon as possible. 'Thank you, Peter, that will do' is much more effective than 'You boy, stop that coughing!', because you are making a personal, polite request, and you have still got the shout in reserve for a real crisis. You can either make the collection of names your first job, pointing round the class and making kids say who they are, or you can do it as they do their first piece of work. Whichever method you employ, before the end of the lesson you need a map of the class-room with every kid's name marked in place, and a clear instruction that they are to sit in the same places until further notice, for the simple reason that you wish to get to know who they are. Show that you mean it by spending time on learning the map, inside lessons and out, and use individual names as much as possible as soon as possible.

As a new teacher at the beginning of the year you are a toy, of immediate interest and with unlimited possibilities. Flattering as this attention may be, your novelty value will soon wear off, and you should not let your natural self-consciousness and the kids' curiosity combine to centre attention on you. They will find out soon enough what you are really like, and a couple of lessons spent in showy self-display will not permanently fool them. While you stand and talk, and expect them to listen, the pressure is on you, and responsibility for the success and failure of the lesson hangs obviously round your neck. So it does in fact, but it is worth hiding it if you can.

The simplest way of relieving yourself of pressure is to put it on the kids, not by shouting at them or threatening, but simply by requiring them to do a piece of work. It may be some form of writing, or answering a questionnaire, but it does need to be unambiguous and within their capabilities. Writing a poem 'suggested' by a piece of music can wait till later in the year – it offers too many loop-holes for misunderstanding. For the moment your concern is to show, not that you are interesting, intelligent or kind, but that you are boss.

Sooner or later, depending on a whole range of factors, you will encounter Noise. Shuffling, muttering, unspontaneous coughing, tapping of pencils on the desk or the snap of a dismembered pen. Do not ignore it, hoping it will go away, or thinking that the beauty of the kids' work will outweigh it; do not throw a fit, threatening to castrate the next kid who coughs – it might be a girl. Instead, notice the interruption, make it clear that you have noticed by a calm look at the kid(s) responsible, and only mention it if you are sure it was deliberate, or if it was provacatively loud. If it happens again, mention it briefly and politely, unless you are sure that it is genuine. If it is obviously hostile, communal and planned, stamp on it quickly. 'I've got a cure for coughing, and it starts at 4 o'clock' is a line I have got away with, but the exact wording must be your choice.

The chances are that the early transgressions will be individual and exploratory, the overtures of 'sniffing out'. If so, respond similarly, one step at a time, keeping as much as possible in reserve for as long as possible. But with all initial disturbances, show that you have noticed them, so that the kids know that your lack of fierce action is simply because you choose not to be fierce, rather than because you have not seen or do not care.

If you do not get one of the Noise moves, you will certainly get the

Equipment gambit as soon as you set any work. This may involve pens, books and jotters initially, but can expand into all sorts of intricate variations. Make sure before you start what school policy is on equipment. Ask: What are kids given by the school? What are they expected to supply themselves? What can you get hold of, and how? In the short term, you can cut out some complications by having spare pens and paper available, but this is a temporary move and must be clearly announced as such, or you will end up supplying the school with biros at an alarming rate. Take a note of who borrows equipment, make sure that it is returned, and keep a record of who is continually without what they are supposed to be with. Some kids do have genuine difficulty in remembering to bring things, but it is very hard to make individual distinctions this early in the game, and you are better off being mean but consistent.

You must also legislate for Movement. Well-bred educationists may not see this as a problem, but they have not played class-room musical chairs, where the kids swap desks whenever the teacher's back is turned, while he desperately tries to remember who was sitting where. It does not get to that stage straight away, but you must ensure that it never does by noting and probably commenting on each movement that takes place. If there is a valid reason, allow it, but make it clear that the movement takes place because you have allowed it, and not simply because you did not notice it.

To some this will smack of dictatorship, and it is true that many teachers wander to windows in summer and heaters in winter, flaunting their privileged mobility in the eyes of their captive pupils. Justice suggests that kids should enjoy the same freedom, but common sense dictates otherwise. There is only one teacher, and thirty kids, and his freedom of movement is much easier to control than theirs. Once encouraged to move, they may saunter round, pay visits, jump on desks and fight, and I have seen them do all four. The simplest precaution is the crudest, that all movement be investigated before it has begun. Investigation need not mean suppression, but it will act as a filter on unthinking disruption. A quiet 'Where are you off to, then?' will produce an answer that can be evaluated and acted upon, according to what you know of the mover and the plausibility of his reason. But the question is useful in its own right, since it tells everyone that you want to know why Jimmy has stood up; potential Jimmies will take note, and not venture to stand up unless they have a reason they think you will accept.

This kind of control, watchful and quiet, needs to be sustained as far as possible through all your early lessons. If the class can become accustomed to you as calm authority, a consistent source of order, they will be far less tempted to subject you to more dire exploration. Although you may resent the effort and pettiness of the campaign, and may feel cheated by the negative image of you which it offers to the kids, you will have the rest of the year in which to show them that you are also interesting and kind. To begin with, they need to know that you are in control, that you will notice, perhaps comment on and finally act against any real challenge to your role as teacher; once they know that, in some detail, you can all relax and get on with the business of education.

It does take more than a lesson. At the end of the first one, therefore, do not yell 'OK, gang, beat it' as you sweep out of the door. That might leave your class with a wonderful impression of your energy and enthusiasm, but it might also leave the next teacher with a floorful of pellets and untidy chairs. So, deliberately finish at least three minutes before the final bell, and make sure that you collect in all equipment issued, if necessary counting books. Not many kids really want to keep a school text book, but quite a few will borrow one for a laugh or leave it stuck behind a radiator. If there is a lot of this kind of tidying up to do (such as, collecting maps, tracing paper, atlases and text books) delegate kids to do it, clearly and politely, and pack up earlier to allow time for it. Most kids are quite happy to do small jobs (although some may need gentle supervision) but all kids like to be free for their breaks on time and so, if you have got any sense, will you. Keep yourself free for general overseer duties, and watch your watch.

Noise, Equipment and Movement, although they all need watching and can each contribute to eventual disaster, will not occupy the bulk of each lesson. What does will depend on the subject taught, and it is vital at this early stage that your preparation should take into account the discipline situation. You need, not lessons which will most amuse or most fully demonstrate your talents or insights, but lessons which will most involve the kids and allow least opportunity for disruption.

In practical subjects, your apparatus is vital. Do everything possible to ensure before the lesson that all you need is in place and working, and be on the lookout for accidents or mischief which might disrupt your plans – projectors unplugged, tape spools borrowed or displays torn down or defaced. Where possible, set up the entire room as you want it before the lesson begins; where it is not possible, do not be harried by the pressure of kids or time into neglecting necessary precautions; better to start five minutes late and go according to plan than to begin with a bang and then find you have forgotten to bring the film. If you have a tight schedule and lose five minutes of it on trivia, try to choose what you will cut out *quickly*; blundering on so that the bell goes in the middle of your carefully prepared climax will spoil the point of the lesson, and they will not revise the whole school's time-table just for you. It is your responsibility to look after the timing of the lesson, and if you do not look after it, no one else will. Finally, if a key practical activity fails completely, forget it as soon as you can, and have something else ready for kids to do. It may well be infuriating, and there may be all sorts of reasons why it is not your fault, but the kids will not want to know about those. If you can turn failure into a useful teaching situation, or can laugh at it happily and carry on regardless, do; but if you cannot, do not try to.

With many lessons, the bulk of your time will be taken up with talking, and if your kids have any life and you intend to teach rather than preach, this means them talking as well as you. In a normal class-teaching situation (as opposed to small groups, or teaching individually) it is essential that only one person talks at a time, and equally essential that the one who talks should not always be the teacher. You therefore need the apparently authoritarian 'hands up' routine, which in my experience kids will accept as a necessary device, and provided it is operated fairly there is no reason why it should inhibit lively and spontaneous discussion. It will not have the freedom, fluency or fire of a 'natural' conversation, but that is the fault of the 1:30 relation-ship and compulsory schooling, not of the 'hands up' routine. With some classes, depending on their past history, it takes time to establish, but that time must be spent. Whatever the strain of appearing too formal and wanting to 'get on', it is worth it as a future investment; once the groundwork has been done, through patience, pauses for explanation and constant practice, you can start the real job of en-couraging contributions and relating comments to each other and previous experience. The alternative, of leaving everything to instinct and the loudest pair of lungs, produces occasional good moments but ultimate anarchy. The quiet kids give up, because they know they will never be heard, the loudest shout quickly and often because they know that is the way to get attention, and you oscillate violently between savage repression and eager enthusiasm, an inconsistency quite as mystifying to the kids as it is wearing for you. Once it has been established, however accidentally and inarticulately, that the way to be heard is simply to yell, you can give up and reach for your ear-plugs.

There will inevitably be interruptions, some of which matter. Some kids' comments are so spontaneous, perceptive or right that they should be allowed to divert discussion – for example, a brief flash of righteous anger from a child who normally says nothing. In that case, I would follow up the interruption, but first placate the speaker interrupted: 'Sorry, Helen, could we follow this up and come back to you in a minute. Yes, Jackie?' This tells all the kids, but especially Helen and Jackie, that you as teacher are deliberately changing the routine, because of something important; you do not leave open the possibility that you are hearing Jackie simply because she is nicer, more intelligent or wearing uniform. Most interruptions, of course, do not come into this *urgent* category; a regular check will show that they come from the same sources, guided far more by personality traits, emotional needs or habit than by relevant compulsion. As a result, I would have a general rule of 'no interruptions' which I would occasionally break, and hardly ever at first. If kids seriously wanted to know why I was breaking it I would try to explain, but otherwise leave it to their sensitivity to understand what was going on.

Chatter is similar. There is useful chatter, harmless chatter and trouble, and only experience or a talented eavesdropper can distinguish between them. Some teachers, and some types of work, require total silence, but others positively demand consultation. Also, in their junior schools and previous lessons in this school, kids will have become accustomed to many varieties of working atmosphere, and it is rare for one to suit all the members of a class. Ultimately, the teacher's approach must be a delicate series of adjustments, compromises and modulations, but to begin with it is easier – and simpler for the kids – to play safe. That does not mean you have to stop every sound that might ever be uttered, which is a very strenuous demand on you, let alone on the kids; it does mean that if you are not sure about something, stop it, and note either by looks or a quiet word that you think the lesson has been interrupted. As usual, personal comments and questions ('What's up, Stephanie?' or 'Yes, Peter?') work a lot better than general exhortation – 'Now then, 3A, there is rather too much noise.' Some classes work well with a constant buzz, and some teachers feel happiest when their room sounds like a factory, but the apprehensive beginner should bear in mind that it is easier to add decibels than to subtract them.

Questions also require the same rigorous scrutiny, and a somewhat sceptical ear. Not all pupil questions are requests for information, and though you may be deeply moved by the upraised hand, earnest face and ever-so-sincere voice, do not judge by appearances alone. The blatant red herrings – 'Did you see *Star Trek*, sir?' – are easy to spot and sometimes fun to follow, but there are more devious versions of which 'Why do we have to do this?' is a common form.

It strikes wickedly at a vulnerable place – the teacher's interest in his own role. He has been trained, he may even have a philosophy, he knows what he is trying to do and why, he owes it to the kids to explain . . . and he is trapped. For he is far more interested in the mechanics of education than his pupils; after all, he *chose* to be there. If he is not careful he will be lost in his own little world of justification, while the kids – their diversion achieved – are happily miles away.

There are genuine questions, of course, and there is no need to deny them or refuse to answer them completely. What they must not do is hold up the course of the lesson unless you are sure that they should. Simply because you are professionally bound to excite and then feed curiosity, the question is the perfect weapon for distraction; it can so easily be camouflaged as the desired product. If you are unsure of a questioner's motives, or feel that the question is genuine but of limited relevance to the class, offer seriously to deal with it at the end of the lesson – real hunger for enlightenment defies even the dreaded bell.

The same applies with defence questions, thrown up in the initial stages of punishment. 'Why do you pick on me?' and 'What about him, miss?' are not always appeals for justice. Kids do have a passionate sense of justice, but they also have a generous allowance of cunning. If you knew that you could evade or postpone punishment by pleading unfairness, would you sit stoically silent and await your fate? Most unlikely. You would probably put on an aggrieved face, say 'it wasn't me' if you thought the teacher had any doubts, and then try to involve as many others as you could, both to disrupt the lesson further and to gain some comforting allies for the time of retribution. From the teacher's point of view it is therefore worth being extremely cautious, and leaving detailed inquiries till later. A genuine grievance can be explored during break-time or after school a lot more intelligently than in the heat of the moment, when an excited, biased jury will be offering their own verdicts and the bell may go at any minute. Sometimes within the limits of the class-room you may have to settle for 'That is just too bad', 'Yes, I am a swine' or total silence, because the alternatives are no more just or decisive, and a lot more threatening to your control.

Expert teachers, of course, are more flexible. They follow red herrings, and then relate them to the original point; they take an alleged injustice and turn it into a class-room trial which is itself an educative experiment; they answer witty repartee with crushing effectiveness and earn trust and affection by their capacity to laugh at themselves and apologise for their mistakes. But such reactions.

although far more attractive and creative than the course of action I have outlined, cannot be learned in a term, and I would earnestly advise any young teacher uncertain of his control in such situations to forget about ideal solutions. There is time to become God's gift to teaching later; for now, survival is the aim.

In my experience, it is through the petty things (pens, desks and shouting out) that trouble comes, so it is through organising them that survival can be achieved. If you can think about, and decide about, the limits of movement or speech you will accept, you will not have to make those decisions again in the pressure of the class-room. This is the point of your teacher-time; using it outside lessons reduces the number of decisions you have to take inside lessons, and therefore cuts your chances of making a five-star blunder. By establishing limits of mobility, recording details of lateness or forgotten equipment, and monitoring the questions you are asked, you will not guarantee great teaching, but you will draw the 'line of control' described in Chapter 8, and this may save you a lot of grief.

In my second year of teaching I had a class which was lively but not genuinely difficult, except for Peter, who was severely disturbed and on his day impossible. When angry he feared no one, was quite prepared to hit anyone who hit him and he had a savage, satirical streak which was clever and highly disruptive. By some miracle he was absent for the first three weeks of the school year, and I spent the time (thanks to an eventful first year) managing to establish the 'line of control' proposed in this chapter, so that it contained virtually the entire class. Peter finally returned, and was surprised to find his mates apparently docile before this new and notoriously incompetent teacher. He took this as a personal challenge, although from conversation with other staff it was clear that his entertaining talents were not confined to English. Most of us had mild crises within weeks of his return.

I managed about as well as most, generally failing with him but contriving to keep my early hold on the rest of the class. They were uneasy, and resentful that he sometimes got away with crimes I would punish them for, but I was not going to encourage them to muck about in the interests of abstract justice.

Eventually, the tension Peter continually carried with him came to a head, and the explosion was enough to convince me that I could not continue to teach Peter one way and the class another; consequently I decided I had to get someone (preferably senior, and free) to look after him, if only for the rest of that shattered lesson. I asked him, in what was meant to be a quiet, firm voice, to go outside the room. He smiled at me angelically, said 'All right', and walked very slowly from the back corner where he always sat, down the gangway between the desks towards me. We watched each other, like opponents in a Western showdown, while the class gave a passable imitation of excited townsfolk waiting, breathless, for the outcome. He thrust his heavily smelling face in front of mine and said 'Give us a kiss.'

Witty improvisers might have done just that, or found the withering crack which would simultaneously deflate him and win over the expectant class. I could not think of one – you never can, at the time – and muttered something weak about 'No thanks . . . now, get out.' He wandered out, much to my relief, and I followed and took him to a senior member of staff who had more time and resource for such a situation.

The discipline problem here was not Peter himself (who, as subsequent events were to show, should not have been placed in a conventional class-room situation at all), but the rest of the class. When I came back they were highly excited, incredulous that I had not hit him, and sure that I had lost. (A friend and colleague had previously hit him, been hit back and had become involved in a nasty show of brute strength over which he lost sleep a week later. He did not 'win' either.) But even though the class was critical of me, and looking for ways in which to exploit my obvious softness, I managed to retain some authority because the memory of a line of control was there. There was a pattern to refer back to, an arrangement familiar to them and to me, to which we could all return after the excitement and real anxiety of the confrontation.

Not all probationer teachers will meet kids like Peter, although some will. But most young teachers will have unplanned crises which blow up suddenly, and never on the days they are ready for them. In such situations, you need something to lean on, some decisions already made, and so do the kids, or one disruption may spark off a whole series of reactions and riots which are difficult to control precisely because they are involuntary. Left to themselves, frightened and excited children will not simply sit still and wait for sir to carry on teaching.

The line of control should be drawn in the first few weeks of a relationship with a class, but it is impossible to say how long that will take or how quickly it can be relaxed. The atmosphere of the school, personalities of staff and pupils and regularity of their lessons together are all highly important variable factors. Clearly, you cannot set up an impeccably ordered framework of ordered activity for three weeks and then throw it all to the winds without unsettling kids and creating as many problems as you would have had without it. On the other hand, a class taught for a whole year with the sole aim of submission will resent it and rightly rebel.

It should, however, be the state of the class which decides the timing of the relaxation rather than the impulses of the teacher. Anyone of any vision or imagination finds it wearing to worry about who has forgotten their pen three weeks on the trot, but that is not an argument for letting everyone do anything for a week. If you are still having trouble maintaining a line of control by Christmas that does not mean you should not have bothered – it is virtual proof that you should. I cannot demonstrate that in an experiment, because teachers, classes and relationships are not replicable, but anyone in doubt should talk to those of us who began teaching without any interest in control. The evidence is chaotic, emotive and highly subjective, but powerful nonetheless.

It is worth emphasising what should be obvious – that the plan of action is a temporary device with a specific aim in view. It is limited, negative, unattractive and insensitive, in that it fails to take full account of individual differences. It treats classes as blocks, contained within subjects and sections of time in a quite unreal way, and it bears no relation to teachers' ideal images of themselves. It is also partial, in that it deals only with one teacher in one class-room, irrespective of the school around him; but that is the view to which most young teachers are restricted. They may well see faults in the régime of the school which intensify their own discipline problems, but they are powerless to change them, and they need, not a blueprint of Jerusalem, but a way of getting by in difficult circumstances.

I do not believe that children are innately vicious or destructive, but think that – like adults – they take much of their behaviour from the patterns in which they have previously lived. If, therefore, most of them have been used to teacher-centred class-rooms governed by a notion of control, they will react uneasily or violently when that control is suddenly removed – watch what happens when a fierce teacher leaves his room for ten minutes. Warfare is not inevitable, but if it is a possibility the teacher must ensure that he will win – for the kids' sakes as well as his own. And if, without silly hysterics or wild threats, he can calmly establish that he will win, the very chance of warfare thereby becomes more remote.

In that knowledge and security, the real task – of establishing relationships, responding genuinely and encouraging real learning – becomes possible. I think many teachers and classes are currently prevented from attempting that task because they are embroiled in power struggles which none of them deeply want. There are various long-term solutions to this, some of which I outline in Part Three of this book; but the simplest short-term solution is to try to increase the rational control of each teacher – and thus give him the base of confidence and order from which the real explorations begin.

The aim of this and the following chapter is to suggest ways in which young teachers can minimise their own misery and reassure their classes, thus accelerating this process; grasping the means of control so as to pass beyond the mere act of control. Faithful application of this chapter will not achieve that end, but use of it as a basis for discussion might help get near it. And if, after all the public debates, philosophical wrangling and private thought, some problems and some kids still emerge as insoluble, that is a humbling but necessary reminder that the whole business, though sophisticated and inevitable, is one gigantic bluff.

Chapter 8

The Teacher's Resources

Talk of survival may sound unduly gloomy, so it is worth reinforcing the proposals of the previous chapter with a detailed reminder of the facilities at the teacher's disposal. These 'resources' extend far beyond the range of printed and filmed material currently indicated by that fashionable label, and make up the repertoire by which most practising teachers ensure their continuing operation and sanity.

Lines of Supply

Firstly, there is a whole collection of apparent trivia, none of which are impressive in isolation but all of which can be manipulated so as to make the job possible – teacher initiative, the setting of work, the mark book, bits of paper and time.

To begin with, you are the teacher. That mere role will not guarantee you permanent respect, but it does mean that you have put more time and thought into what happens than anyone else in the room. You have been trained, expensively if not thoroughly, and you occupy a position from which class-room activity traditionally springs. You cannot simply relax because of that, but it does give you a valuable initiative; they may not come in wanting to obey or dying to learn, but they will expect you to say and do things so that, to begin with at least, you have their attention. Whether you keep it will depend on how well you use that initiative, and how ruthless they are in 'sniffing out', but it is there when you start your first lesson.

You also have a more lasting initiative, although this depends on your department and can at times be a dubious privilege, in that you decide in advance what is meant to happen. No kid will spend as much time as the teacher planning his next encounter, and that is a kind of advantage. At the beginning, I would use it negatively, by avoiding the areas of potential discipline risk (free movement around the class, unsupervised group work, private research in lessons but out of sight), but as mutual confidence develops it can become more positive, as experiment and variation relieve the class-room pressure and enable you to talk with kids more freely.

In my first year of teaching, in my second lesson with 3W, I resolved to give them a foretaste of the joys they had in store; no more stuffy dictations or copying off the board, we were going to do *plays* today! It was an afternoon double, and I must have been crazy. They were not used to small-group drama, I was not used to teaching it and I had not a really clear idea of what I wanted. A couple of the plays were not bad, and there was not a riot, but they did get used to wandering round, chattering idly without any real purpose, *almost as soon as they had met me.* It does not take a genius to make the association (English = do what you like) and you can predict what happened later. At the time, it seemed an innocent miscalculation; now, I think it was disastrous.

This does not mean that you cannot experiment with difficult kids. You can, and it is exciting, valuable and often necessary to do so, but such experiment does not have to take place in the first few days of term. I have personally done bigger, better and far more ambitious work since, and with far more difficult kids, by waiting until they had had time to get used to me and my ways, and vice versa.

I would therefore advise using your powers of planning to avoid such risks for at least three weeks, maybe longer. I would advise the same about open friendliness with a really rough class, and for the same reason; they need to get used to you. It is tempting, if you have been frustrated by your teacher-training and are eager to tackle the nitty-gritty of 'real' teaching, to want to demonstrate your full talent and love all at once; in many schools, too, the dead weight of repressive tradition weighs down on your class-room, so that the need to combat it with sympathy and freedom seems urgent. Nonetheless, the kids you are teaching are probably used to different patterns; they have had a colossal variety of teachers before you, and smiles and discussions on the first day may well signal to them that you are simply soft and do not mind what they do.

I am advising caution, therefore, for practical reasons. I do not believe that 'You have to go slowly' in all forms of change, and I am sure that perpetual caution is quite as destructive as perpetual haste. But in this situation, because of the way the kids will see you, I think it is worth advancing slowly. That need not mean monotony or boredom for them, although it may mean impatience and momentary guilt for you; yet they know, subconsciously but still better than you do, that they have got you for a year and fireworks in September do not mean a thing. They will not switch off for good if your first four lessons are not exciting (although they probably will moan and compare you unfavourably with other teachers), and even if you get to

Christmas without having shown them your full talents, there is still two-thirds of the year to go – and about ninety terms after that. It may well be easier in the long run to be thought dull and strict in October than stunning on 1 September; what, you need to ask yourself, will they think of me by the end of June?

Once you have chosen the work, and decided that those particular kids can usefully do it, set it clearly; say what you want slowly, and if you are not sure of their attention write it on the board before the lesson begins – if they will not listen while you are talking you certainly cannot afford to turn your back. Allow time for questions, but deal with them carefully and methodically, answering hands rather than shouts. If possible, ensure that this above all else satisfies the 'one-at-a-time' routine, and make the replies loud enough for everyone to hear. That way, when a kid says 'Which page, sir?' after you have said it three times, you *know* he is mucking you about. Do not let questions roll on for ever, and impose a guillotine if it looks as though they are being used to postpone work indefinitely.

It is in specific instances like the setting of work (or asking questions, or punishment) that teacher language is important to discipline. Heretically, I do not think that the study of language is the key to all educational problems, and with discipline hostile or impersonal forms of address are often reflections of personality or attitude rather than merely verbal phenomena. In the process of setting work, however, it is worth paying attention to the words you use. Avoid polysyllabic asides, whether intended wittily or as illustration of your erudite training – a kid who asks 'How do I start?' does not want to be told, 'Blenkinsop, you exhibit tendencies which are positively Aristotelian.' It might amuse you, but to him it is either irrelevant or insulting, and therefore a distraction. Keep to the point, and if there are difficult words that you cannot avoid using, find a way of explaining them to everyone which does not expose slow kids to ridicule.

When the work is done, mark it. That means collect it in, read it and then write something which shows that you have read it. Your comment, mark or tick is an index of your awareness; if you never check to see that all the books are in, do not comment on lazy work, do not praise real effort and do not regret squandered talent, you are effectively saying that you do not care. The buzz of creation within your brain, and the high-powered project you are going to launch next Thursday, are worthless if Johnny is getting the message that you do not mind whether he does fifteen pages or nothing. Being human, he will probably do nothing, and he certainly will not pull out all the stops in class if he knows that the lad behind has not written a thing for four weeks and has not heard a peep from you. Failure to mark is thus not only inefficient but dangerous. For the child's recognition that you are indifferent to his work will not simply stop there, at idle, mutual lack of interest. Since he is forced to be in your lesson, he will come and devise some form of revenge, some way of making you notice him, and this is unlikely to take polite or desirable forms. So, in your own interests as well as for more noble motives, mark.

Your best friend in this is your mark book. It is of no great significance, of course, whether Johnny got $7\frac{1}{2}$ or 8 in your last test, or whether this is Mary's eighth or ninth consecutive 9 out of 10, and in consequence many teachers despise mark books as a relic from the ancient past. They do, however, have their uses, since a mark book may be the teacher's sole check on who has done *anything*; and while it may not matter that Josie's got 9 when Eric's got $1\frac{1}{2}$, it matters a lot if Billy's done nothing for half a term. To the teacher, a thick wad of books may suggest that he is getting somewhere – '19 out of 30, not bad for this lot' – but if Billy's is never in that wad then Billy will know, and act accordingly. He may turn sulky, despite the teacher, or positively glory in his undiscovered sloth, but none of these responses will help either Billy or the teacher, and some of them will disturb other kids. So, keep a mark book and tick who has done what.

As a notebook rather than an adding machine, the mark book is a useful record. Continuous assessment of some kind is even better, but this is hardly common practice and it does take a lot of work and time. But whatever your system, you will certainly need other pieces of paper; just as the mark book may tell you (and then later remind you) exactly which three boys have not handed in their homework, so other words on paper can eventually save you from a nervous breakdown. You need as a minimum something, apart from your head, which will tell you instantly:

what you are going to do next lesson;
when you are going to set homework, and what;
who owes you work or punishments from previous lessons;
who did not have required equipment last time.

In the class-room, at crisis points when you are least capable of rational thought, you are going to want to know something which only two days ago was blindingly obvious. During those two days, however, so much has happened, so many books, incidents and kids have passed through your life, that you have entirely forgotten which five girls you told to stay in yesterday lunchtime, and who were the two who turned up. If they know you have forgotten, you have had it; if you pick on the two who came, they will pull the school down; if you ask the whole class they 'cannot remember'; if you let them all go you have lost; if you have got a little list, you have a chance.

Paper thus creates breathing space, saving the memory so as to leave your battered brain clear for supervision and critical decisions. It can also be a direct help in confrontation, checking excitement by its suggestion of objective permanence. At the end of one lesson I wanted to get rid of a gang of near-hysterical fourth-year girls, so that I could talk to one of them on her own. The others, giggling and virtually help-less, said they were going to stay. 'Right,' I said firmly, 'I am asking you to leave. Now,' deliberately getting out pen and paper, 'who insists on staying?' The prospect of a list of names was somehow more threatening than teacher possibly getting mad, so they went. In itself the mere writing down of names is no more ominous than a verbal threat, but it does seem to carry a kind of tribal magic with it. Also, like the policeman's caution, it formally indicates seriousness, and is a good diversion if you have bumped into a crook you do not know – take his name and number (form, house or tutor set) and then at least you can find him again if you need to. Like everything else, the mere act of writing down details is not instantly or universally effective and can be overdone, but it can also help.

Teacher-time, I argued in Chapter 5, is the decisive factor in many discipline situations, and the young teacher should hoard his time like Yukon gold. In my own first year I lost some confrontations simply because I had to leave school early to catch a lift, and though some demands like that may be unavoidable you should resist all the claims on your time that are not. For instance, only the headmaster is statutorily required to exercise responsibility over pupils at lunchtime, so it may be important for a young teacher to politely turn down the chance to do a dinner duty, even though some schools still present it as a virtual obligation.

Extra-curricular activities, too, need watching. They do perform the dual function of impressing headmasters while allowing you to make contact with kids outside lessons, and this can be a precious relief from the artificial warfare of the class-room. Also, they can occasion-ally be a positive help, in allowing you to make sympathetic contact with a kid who in the context of lessons is withdrawn or hostile. In a large comprehensive, too, there are likely to be enough lively young staff to build up a highly attractive subculture, which can sometimes

I

tempt you to commit large amounts of time simply as an escape from the pressure of actual teaching.

But although I have done a fair amount of this myself, and loved it, I would again counsel caution. The gains and enjoyment of work outside school are tremendous, but they do not alter your basic time-table commitment to thirty-five lessons a week, and it is that which justifies your presence. Once you have signed away your precious time to a whole range of good causes, it is very difficult decently to reclaim it when you want to – a month after the beginning of term, when you have just had a riot and need to keep kids in. Intelligently used, time outside lessons can relieve the pressures inside lessons, in at least two ways. Firstly, you need occasional safety valves, times when you force yourself to relax, chat in the staff-room or go out for a walk or drink. Secondly, you can take practical steps to make future lessons easier, in ways that you could not predict at the beginning of the year. You may need, as I did, to spend lunchtimes writing on the blackboard, duplicating worksheets, arranging piles of paper, counting pens, sorting through old lists, or preparing punishments which you think you are going to need. You may need to do those things, sordid and petty as they are, or you may not, but you should not commit your lunch-times till you are sure.

Analysis

If you care about what you are doing, and want to make yourself better at the job before you have a baby, emigrate or become a head-master, you will have to spend some time thinking about what you are doing and how you could improve. There are teachers, some of them young, who really do pack up at 4.00 p.m. and do not think about school until 9.00 a.m. next day, but they are generally neither effective nor happy in their work; for most of us it is necessary, and sometimes enjoyable, to use some evenings and weekends analysing where we are going wrong.

I can remember spending three hours one night looking through a variety of poems, just to find the right one which would help me win back a nice lively class I had lost by a stupidly casual lesson earlier that day – most of the sickest trouble comes from taking something for granted. As it happened, I need not have bothered; both they and I were so determined to be rid of our smouldering unpleasantness that the next day's lesson would probably have gone well in any case, but I was not to know that. It was still worth spending three hours in trying to make thirty-five minutes the next day a bit more bearable.

That disproportion suggests that there have to be limits, and there have to be lessons which have not been planned as thoroughly as you might like. But although you must set limits on your involvement, and fiercely retain a private life with which school has nothing to do, it is worth being very careful also about how you spend your preparation time, and which classes it goes on. The normal pattern is to devote most attention to the classes which cause most trouble, and that is fair enough; what usually happens is that after a period of neglect a class which you thought was easy becomes restive, and so you concentrate on them, thus eventually working to a subconscious but reasonable rota of attention. But in day-to-day planning there is a more dangerous tendency, to plan lessons in the order in which you will teach them, from 1 to 8 throughout the day. The danger here is that if you get fed up with preparation you will decide to improvise the later lessons, or (optimistically) plan them as you teach in the morning, and they are exactly the ones that are most likely to go wrong. More riots happen between 3.00 p.m. and 4.00 p.m. than between 9.00 a.m. and 10.00 a.m., because riots come from tiredness, tension and a lack of clear thinking. It is almost worth, therefore, planning your lessons in exactly reverse order, so that the early part of your preparation time (and the maximum of your remaining energy) goes on averting afternoon chaos; if you *have* to 'get by', it is easier to do so while they are still hungry for lunch.

Apart from planning, you need time for retrospective analysis. Teaching practice should have accustomed you to the interplay of theory and action, noting good points and trying to repeat them, recognising mistakes and seeking to eliminate them, looking regularly at your work, class by class, to see how it is going. In the first year of full teaching, however, such a process is even more urgent – and twice as difficult. There is no guiding hand to blame if things go wrong, no special provision by the school to shield you from the worst blows, and the earliest likely end to the ordeal is twelve months away rather than a few weeks. It is only the stupid and the arrogant, therefore, who dispense with analysis completely.

It does need, though, to be positively done, or it degenerates into an arid self-pity, understandable but useless. The key is to translate 'trouble' – that vague, subjective agony – into specific, objective factors. For example, does 'I can't do anything with 4B' mean 'They are always fighting', 'They will not shut up when I tell them to' or 'They never do any written homework'? If all three, pick the most important and tackle it, or deal with each of them one at a time, but isolate *something* and decide on your next appropriate move. No, of course

I am not that cool when kids get me mad, but I try to be, and when I can manage it I find an answer a lot faster.

The same applies to the '5X are hell' feeling, which needs breaking down into particularity: All of 5X? If not, which ones, and for what reasons? Who is the most disruptive, and when? Are there any obvious reasons in your lesson for such behaviour? Are they like that with other teachers? What changes might alter the way they act? Are those changes within your power? (If not, it is not your fault; if they are, make them.) Always, tackle the general feeling with particular questions and make yourself give specific answers; if it is easier, talk with a friend and get him to do it, but do not just sit there wallowing in the masochistic luxury of 'Kids are bastards, school is hell and I cannot cope.' All those are true some of the time, but none of them are for ever.

'The truth of the situation is the truth for the child' in discipline as much as in learning, and the teacher's feeling about a lesson is not sufficient guide as to how that lesson has gone. You need to assess your own performance just as rigorously as you would a kid's piece of work, and this means looking at it from different points of view. The crucial question afterwards is not the breathless 'How did it go?' or 'How do I feel?', but 'What did that mean for John . . . or Julie . . . or Sharon?'

With discipline, in your first year of teaching in a comprehensive, the answers will not be brilliant. It may be 'that was the lesson I stopped John strolling round the room' or 'that was the lesson I made Julie stay behind and say what she was giggling about' or 'that was the lesson there was enough silence for Sharon to say something in a class discussion'. These will not sound world-shaking to people outside teaching and they probably were not the goals suggested by philosophy lectures, but in this territory it is the trivia that matter .

Particular actions, therefore, rather than general feelings. Fear, anger or guilt are powerful emotions, but they are reactions to crises and not solutions. The longer they last, the more they postpone the decisions and actions which might change the situation, so that although you cannot help feeling down now and again, that very feeling ought to be recognised from the beginning as a threat. Telling yourself you are a lousy teacher feeds a hungry conscience but does not do a thing for the kids you are trying to teach, and letting them know the effect they are having on you will make things worse rather than better.

It is common for classes to hound teachers into tears, give them presents and apologies next day, and then persecute them again the following week. Kids who in calm moments, on their own, are charming, sensitive and kind can in an uncontrolled situation become part of a vicious, merciless gang, and the power of the emotions they release (in both themselves and the teacher) may frighten them but rarely holds them back. This abrupt change, sometimes touching and sometimes heart-breaking, is not due to any conscious deceit; in the clear light of day they really are sorry and do not mean to do it again, but if real trouble starts they will not be able to help themselves.

This suggests that answers will have to come from the teacher rather than from the class, and although the exact nature of the answer can only be worked out in the class-room, its general direction can and should be established by careful, specific analysis of what went wrong last time. You will not find immediate solutions to everything, but then you cannot really expect to master a complex and demanding job within a year. All you can do, and should do, is to work out what your lessons mean for different kids (and do not always pick the same ones each time), and what it might be in those lessons which makes the kids bored, restless or rude. Use overheard comments when they are useful ('I am sick of poems, why do we always do poems?') but do not treat them as gospel or torture yourself by brooding on the worst ones; 'this is boring' and 'why can't we have Miss Wilson back?' are hurtful but unhelpful, and therefore are not worth remembering. Kids will come out with all sorts of comment during the day (just as you will) and you should not select a particularly searing or complimentary example as 'what the kids think'. You are doing a job, and you probably know more about it than they do; if they can help, and make specific suggestions which it is useful to follow, well and good, but the only person who really *must* think about what is going on in your room is you. You decide what happens, and though it will not be perfect it should be the best you can do; neither your headmaster nor your conscience can ask for more.

Crisis

The best lesson plans of teachers and students gang aft agley, and although analysis is vital over the year it will not guarantee you silent classes. Whatever your preparations or talents, there may well be times when you find yourself stuck or afraid. What can you do?

Firstly, stay put. However restless you feel, sit at the teacher's desk and make kids come to you. This puts them through the ritual of recognising that you are in charge, and the physical demarcation of the table-top can be quite powerful. Also, that arrangement allows you to keep everyone else in sight while you talk to one individual. The sudden charge across the room may feel impressive, but you have got to be a good actor to sustain it, and while you are glowering over a crook you have not a clue what is happening behind you. Also, you have got to find a way of getting back to base with dignity, whereas if you stay put that becomes someone else's problem.

Do not shout unless you really have to – a really wild kid, a full-scale riot where kids genuinely would not hear anything softer, or a potentially dangerous fight. Shouting as a regular gambit commits you to competition (they have to shout to keep talking to each other, you shout louder to get over that, etc., etc.), from which quiet kids will withdraw entirely. More important still, you are bound to lose, since there are thirty of them, they can rest when they want to and you talk more than they do over the day as a whole. Besides that, many kids deeply resent being yelled at, and I do not blame them. There are teachers who live on a permanent megaphone level, but it requires massive lungs and regular exercise.

A simple pause can often be more effective, when you wait for some decrease in row and then repeat, quietly and slowly, what you were saying. It is not instant, and can be overdone, but it creates a seed of doubt about what you are going to do; shouting makes that all too clear, and they will not want to know. In crisis, the tendency is to try to rush towards a solution, getting louder and faster; resist it, and slow down.

Most things in this field are subject to the law of diminishing returns, and losing your temper is no exception. There will be times when you just cannot help it, but at such times you are hardly likely to be thinking about this or any other book; when you can help it, do. For although a spontaneous outburst may be shatteringly effective once (stunned silence, followed by stage whisper – 'I did not know he had it in him'), it is a currency liable to devaluation. As a routine it becomes entertaining rather than a serious aid to control – 'Ey, sir, you do not half twist your mouth funny when you are mad.'

Do not discuss a crisis situation with a class. This will sound like bland deception, but the kids are not as interested in discipline analysis as you are, and to tell them they are troubling you will only increase their sense of power and make things worse. For instance, if one boy's behaviour makes it essential to change the course of a lesson, make it look as though that was what you were going to do anyway. The alternative – 'We were going to do X, but because Ralph's being a twit we cannot' – may make you feel temporarily better but will not help. The implicit appeal to class disapproval as an agent of discipline rarely works, and when it does can be a nasty form of buck-passing. Even worse, by bringing the discipline situation out into the open you make two damaging confessions: to Ralph, you say that he has succeeded in controlling your lesson, and can do so any time he dislikes what is going on; to the rest of the class, you admit that he has done it, that you are powerless to stop him and cannot teach as you want. Both admissions may be true, but it will not help to advertise them.

Try to prevent trouble spreading, both to innocent kids and to other classes. If a group is being troublesome, do not keep the whole class in; if one class has mucked you about, try to prevent that from disrupting your next lesson – in other words, do not carry on a running legal battle when you have got other kids to teach. If you want to punish kids, arrange to see them later, at a time convenient to you, but do not load the odds against yourself by making impossible demands; keeping a whole class in from 4.00 p.m. till 4.30 p.m. in total silence will probably put far more strain on you than it will on them. Try, therefore, to limit your pockets of real trouble to the times, places and kids that you have chosen.

If a lesson starts badly, try to take the crucial discipline decisions as early as possible; unless you have something good prepared, it will get worse before it gets better, and the later you leave real action the more likely you are to utter impossible threats or commit yourself to something stupid. If the pressure on you is building up, try to spread it, but gently, on the kids; do not shout at them, or make them sit still with their hands on their heads, because if they have anything about them they will use that to make your life even more impossible. Give them something to do, probably writing, which requires minimum explanation; imply by the way you announce it that it is the work you wanted to do next anyway, and try not to suggest that you know a crisis is looming up. Give out pens and papers if you have to, but create a situation as fast as possible where each kid has a clear, long piece of work to do and the means to do it, and where you are free to watch them all and to think about your next move.

The temptation for any leader is to do the opposite, to keep talking or shouting until opposition ceases or the enemy goes home. Headmasters often adopt this technique with critical staff meetings, but they only get away with it because staff are handicapped by their politeness. Kids in a crisis will suffer from no such restraints, and a long harangue will only offend the angels, bore the middle-of-the-road kids, and amuse the crooks no end. So, keep the speech-making to a minimum, and as soon as possible find something to take their attention off you and power, and onto themselves and work.

Finally, if you really must, use other staff. It is not a pleasant move, and many staff-rooms by their casual conversation treat a request for help as tantamount to an admission of impotence. But it may be better than carrying on in lonely despair; it may also provide another authority figure for the kids, which will help them return to rough normality – once excited, few classes have the power to control themselves, and a new face is often a helpful catalyst. Try to pick a member of staff who is near, effective and at least partially sympathetic, and have something specific to give him – 'Robert Jackson has just broken this chair' is a lot more use than 'Please do something, I just cannot cope.' This may, of course, be unfair on Robert Jackson, in that it is your riot rather than his, but the priority is to get the class within control rather than to achieve absolute justice immediately. Getting someone else in will of course diminish your status in the eyes of many kids and some staff, but it is not the end of the world.

Very few things are, in fact. In retrospect, I am amazed at the disasters one can survive as a teacher, and most kids have a similar resilience. You make mistakes, of course, and they do suffer from them, but if you work at it and think about what you are doing you really do get better very quickly. That is little consolation in a tough first term, when 'very quickly' means two minutes rather than two years, but at such times it is worth attempting a long-term view so as to put the immediate anguish of failure in perspective.

Sanctions

Only a few people actually enjoy punishing kids, but fewer still manage to get through a useful teaching career without any resort to it at all. And to young teachers, whose own school memories may supply hopelessly inadequate examples of crime and punishment, one of the most urgent questions is 'What can you do?'

The mere fact that that question can be posed does not mean that it can be satisfactorily answered, and although some like to talk as if there used to be 'a real answer', I doubt if any generation of teachers has ever been entirely confident about the morality and effectiveness of the sanctions imposed in their schools, and those most sure of their rightness are probably those most in need of doubt. Punishing people ought to make you feel uneasy; the real problems come when it is a routine or a pleasure. With the proviso, then, that there is no logical reason why there should be an exactly appropriate penalty for every crime, it is worth reviewing the teacher's armoury.

Firstly, conventional weapons, like telling a kid his behaviour is unworthy of the school, his house or his form, his family or himself; the deduction of merits or awarding of black marks, whether personal or as part of a house system; or the teacher's disapproval, conveyed by a lecture in front of the class or a malign entry in the mark book. All these are hallowed by tradition, highly respectable and quite useless.

Moving into the real world, the teacher can offer a straight telling off, which if it is brief will only be adequate for very young kids or for those who have acted temporarily out of character. Kids fidgeting, fighting or distracting each other can be threatened with physical separation; and that, like all threats, has to be remembered and kept to if it is ignored. If you can, threaten what you might do and also explain afterwards why you have done it – both in private if possible. This allows a chance for examining genuine grievances, and shows that you are not simply acting out of anger or hate. Some teachers send individual children out of the room, but this has to be done very carefully; with younger kids it may well be a brief shock which kicks them out of a giggling fit, but it will not have a serious effect on serious problems. It is an immediate relief for the poor, harassed teacher, but probably short-lived. For unless the crook has been given a specific task and suitable place in which to do it, where the teacher can check up on what he is doing (at the risk of neglecting the rest of the class) he will probably wander off for a walk or make faces through the window. Even if he just sits there doing nothing, getting bored and wandering away when the bell goes, he will have got the message that the teacher does not want to know about him, and that may spell trouble later on. The cooler customers will welcome the chance of a breather – I know one fourth-year girl who persistently talks every time she feels shut in by a maths lesson, because she knows she will be able to wander off for a walk when she is sent out.

In extreme cases, where a child simply cannot be contained within the class-room and there is no overall framework of discipline to which you can turn, it is possible to sit him alone with a lot of work, and to check on progress later, but it takes time to do it effectively. Sending out is a preliminary to an individual talk, another punishment or the setting of a specific assignment; in itself it is of very limited value.

Ideally, punishments should be related to the crime involved: doing a poor piece of work again, scrubbing a desk covered with ink, paying for damage caused, making someone walk back slowly down a corridor he has just run down (which will sound extremely petty, except to teachers whose rooms adjoin popular corridors). Craft workshops and PE storerooms seem to provide inspiration for the setting of the most obscurely ingenious punishments, but these are valued more for the amusement they offer staff than for their sense or deterrent value.

As an English teacher, I am against using essays as a punishment simply to suggest a deterrent or teacher disapproval, because it indicates that all work is an authoritarian imposition, with no clear distinction between English (what we are here for, something worth doing) and punishment (an extra, because of some offence). There is in this sense a case for deliberately senseless punishments, in that they demonstrate to staff and kids a clear, deliberate waste of time. Trying to humanise the process of retribution can lead to ridiculous contradictions, where kids given interesting jobs to do as a punishment come back next day to ask if they can do them again.

If you want to punish someone in a purely vengeful sense the easiest method is reporting, where you tell a kid to stand outside the staff-room for whatever number of lunchtimes or breaks appeals. This saves precious teacher-time, in that you only need to nip out occasionally to see if he is still there, and it does encroach on a kid's time, thereby affecting him. That may not sound much, but it is sometimes hard to find measures which will actually affect the child, rather than merely expressing your own anger and frustration. Punishment in school must be punitive, deterrent or symbolic, since the supposed remedial aim of adult imprisonment does not apply – kids will be in school and receiving 'treatment' anyway. Fining them presents problems, hitting them is controversial, locking them up is a little archaic (although not entirely outmoded), and so the most frequent method is to deprive the kid of his time through detention.

Detention comes in two forms, school and private. For a school detention there is a rota of teachers responsible for supervision, and the punishing class teacher signs a book or fills in a form to say whom he has placed in detention and why. This sounds fine, a wide sharing of discipline responsibility throughout the school, but it usually works very badly. Many teachers who do not or will not use the system resent having to supervise other teacher's crooks, and it often develops into a weak habit for a few junkies who put in half a dozen kids a day and get no better discipline as a result. The process of checking whether one particular kid has turned up is extremely complicated in a school of any size and the actual supervision, though it may occur rarely, is either a tiresome chore or a nightmare – for a detention class will be a hand-picked gang of crooks, probably well-known to each other and certainly resentful at having their free time taken away. If the teacher supervising them is known to be less than confident they will be more than happy to provide him with yet another riot. Finally, excessive use of a school detention results in a farce whereby teachers queue up for an appointment with especially 'popular' villains, and if your chosen victim is in detention every night for a week it is highly unlikely that by the time next Thursday comes around he will remember what he is in for, let alone that it was you who put him in. I had one friend so depressed by the fatuity of the exercise that he ran one detention as a free discussion lesson, chatted happily to the amazed kids and then sent them home after ten minutes.

Much more effective is the private detention, where the link between crime and punishment is much closer and more clearly established. In this, you decide on a time when you want to keep particular kids in, warn them of it and sift through any excuses very carefully, and then supervise them yourself. The numbers must not be large, and you must know before you start where you want them to sit and what you want them to do – repeat a bad piece of work, copy out a dictionary, sit and gaze straight ahead, learn poems off by heart, or whatever. Add time on for kids who try to disrupt the detention (having warned them first that you will) and do not give in if they look sad and pathetic on their own. All sorts of kids who are loud and insufferable in the class-room shrink dramatically when deprived of friends and allies, but if you have started even a little war you must make sure that you win. If you do let them go early because you are sorry for them, you can bet they will run off to their friends, gleeful that you are so soft, and will play hell with your next lesson. It is a merciless business.

The value of the private detention is that you remain the responsible adult, obviously controlling the situation, and that the time spent will intrude into the kid's life. In the imperfect situation you are both in, you as teacher must find a short-term way of intruding, of making a difference to the kid, and making him lose half-an-hour of his lunchtime will probably do that. You do not need to stand over him threatening – in fact it is probably more effective if you suggest calm remoteness, coolly marking other books while your subjects carry out your will; the punishment is not your displeasure but the time he is losing. Finding such a lever, a threat which will matter enough *to the kid* to make a difference, can be much, much more subtle than you would think; I once threatened a class that if they did not stop interrupting the peculiarly soulful piece of work I was attempting they could sit and copy things off the board. 'All right', was the almost unanimous reply, and I watched helplessly as they cheerfully copied. Useless, time-wasting and a kind of interlude, but certainly no punishment – and no education either.

The most obvious way of intruding into a child's life, however, is to hit him. We have done this for so long that we have forgotten what a strange accompaniment it makes to rational persuasion and mental development, and how easily other countries manage without it. However, the habit is there, and the fact that teachers and pupils are aware of it as a possibility creates more problems than a simply satirical or propagandist approach can cure. There are two main forms of hitting kids, or – to use the protective euphemism – corporal punishment: (1) caning, which is legal, highly formal, and in decreasing use; and (2) belting, which is illegal, immediate and much more widespread than many people like to pretend.

Caning I can see no use for. The regulations governing the ritual are so elaborate (amount of time elapsed since offence, black book to be signed, measurement of cane, signature of witnesses, etc.) as to deprive it of what little meaning it ever had. The kid will either be terrified out of his wits (it is invariably a him, for some reason) or bitterly resigned to the proceedings, but in neither case will the experience have much useful effect upon his character or conduct. 'It never did me any harm', the advocates cheerily affirm, but if it did no harm it probably did no good either, for the theory behind it is that by sudden controlled violence it makes a lasting difference to behaviour. If this were so, the ideal candidates for the cane would be minor crooks aged 11 or 12, most susceptible to the 'short, sharp shock', but soft-hearted teachers seem instead to opt for fourth-year boys, the same scruffy old group they caned last time and will go on caning for as long as the law allows.

The strongest support for the cane, in fact, seems to derive from its symbolic value. It is a sudden, dramatic gesture, representing to possible wrongdoers and the watching world that a line has been drawn – *this* we will not have. Some such justification must lie behind the passionate defences made of it; 'But we must have *something*', they say, or 'Well, what else is there? What is the answer?' There is absolutely no reason why there should be any answer; the universe was not constructed on the principle that teachers should at all times be able to think of convenient punishments, and the statistics of the cane's use show clearly that it is no more 'the answer' than anything else. The cane is, however, potently '*something*', and it is the fear of 'nothing' which underlies its determined retention by many staff.

Informal belting is more interesting, although more difficult to discuss as in theory it does not exist. There are obvious reasons why teachers should not be allowed to treat kids entirely as they like, but a quick blow in a fit of rage, or in response to open insolence, is a lot more understandable than the ritual of a legal caning. In the words of the teacher's cliché – 'Never hit a child except in anger.'

Some swipes or taps can act as correctives to a silly mood, but it is hard to draw precise guidelines, and kids react in very different ways. The times when you are most tempted to hit kids are also the times when you are least in a position to judge what you are doing, and as a rule the kids you are most tempted to hit are the ones least likely to be usefully affected. That unlikely result is, very occasionally, possible: Farley, in *Secondary Modern Discipline*, describes an incident in which a boy shoved an elderly teacher so as to make him fall over, promptly received a right hook from a younger teacher, and was apparently valuably chastened by the experience. For some kids in some situations, such a move might in fact be less sadistic than a moralistic lecture or protracted inquisition; whatever the verbally oriented assumptions of educational theory, not all physical contact is worse than all verbal contact, and for some teachers and some kids belting may well be a natural, accepted mode of expression.

It is not for me, however, and the fact that it is for some does not mean that anything goes, or that because little Harry is knocked around at home he therefore ought to get knocked around at school 'because that is the only language his sort understands'. If it really is, he ought logically to be allowed to hit teachers back, but few staff will carry their logic that far. For a kid who is regularly hit at home, in fact, being hit at school may well be expected but will almost certainly not be effective, and we do as teachers have some responsibility to suggest a mutually respectful relationship, even if we cannot always manage it. For myself, I would want to get by without hitting kids, and I would certainly advise any probationer very strongly against it, for legal reasons as well as many others.

But there are schools where classes are so fragmented and an overall pattern so dramatically absent that a young teacher left to sink or swim may feel he has to resort to drastic measures. Occasions do arise, usually because of your own stupidity, when there just does not seem to be any alternative; I can recall hitting a kid who told me to drop dead, and seeing what I swear was relief on his face, that there actually was a limit to how far my ludicrous softness would go. I know teachers who have ascribed their success with a difficult class to one violent confrontation early in the year, after which there was no trouble of any kind. I used to think that my own first year might have been easier if I had hit the right three boys in the first week; the snag was, at that stage I would not have known whom to hit, or when, or how. If you know the really crucial incidents, and the battles you dare not lose, you are not really in trouble anyway and should not need to hit anyone. If you must, make sure that (*a*) you are prepared to face the legal and practical consequences; (*b*) you can live with your conscience; (*c*) there is not a better way of quelling that particular kid; (*d*) it will make long-term relationships with the class as a whole better rather than worse. If you really can satisfy all those conditions, you are lucky. If you cannot, or you are not sure, wait.

Ultimate sanctions like suspension are beyond your province. The range you have at your disposal is limited, negative and archaic, and complicated by a confusion of motives it is very hard to disentangle. Are you trying to interest the kid, frighten him or bore him? Does it matter what other kids think of how you punish one of their classmates? Can you effectively punish groups, who laugh when they are kept together and complain of unfairness when they are split up? What, really, 'works'?

The question comes back, as it must, to be solved by each individual out of his own experience. All I would offer is one other device, which may or may not be a punishment, and which demonstrates not only the ambiguity of the whole penal discussion but also the possibilities of more positive contacts. This is the chat.

The chat takes place with one kid, or two if they are really close and can talk to you without being funny with each other and thus undermining you. If in doubt, see them one at a time. Conditions will vary, but must involve you and the kid, in a room on your own (that is without eavesdroppers at doors, spectators at windows or stowaways in cupboards, any one of whom will affect the atmosphere), at a time when you are not meant to be doing anything else; that is, when the kid knows that you want to see him, and you are not supposed to be teaching half a mile away.

The chat may take two minutes, when you simply wish to say something brief and forceful, leaving it to him or to her to think about it; or it may start at the beginning of a lunch hour, so that you can go on for half an hour if the kid is either rudely obstructive or eager to talk. I had a friend who once spent an entire double free lesson talking with a girl who had rudely interrupted his lesson and refused to apologise. Needless to say, they wandered on to other things in the course of conversation, but they talked for the whole hour; later, she apologised, 'but only because he is nice'. Whatever the original purpose of the chat (unless the kid specifically asks to talk to you) let the time and place be your choice; preserve your breaks as breathing spaces if you can, and if you have told a particular kid to see you at a particular time, do not be conned out of it or allow yourself to forget it if he does not turn up. Yet again, the question is not how you feel (fed up with the whole dreary business) but what he thinks. If what you have said and done does not touch him at all, he has no reason to change his behaviour.

This criterion would rule out many of the lectures and sermons which currently pass for 'a telling-off', since they are in fact monologues composed and delivered by the teacher, and only fully understood by him. True, the sheer length and volume of a tirade can be a punishment, but a crude one, and if you turn words on like a cold shower you cannot expect to get anything back. Exactly what form your chat takes must depend on its purpose, but it should be long enough and open enough to make the kid feel he is involved; a simple question is often a good start, provided it is clear and can reasonably be expected to provide an answer – 'Why are you so stupid?' will not be a good beginning, but 'You were a bit daft today, weren't you?' might be. 'Yes' leads to exploration of the kid's mood, his comments on the lesson and what it did not offer him, your reminder of the class as a whole and their needs, a joint discussion of the likelihood of the daftness being repeated, and so on. 'Dunno' leads to a closer look at what he actually did to incur your wrath, while 'No' could do the same, or else could lead to a general view of the kid's life in school via 'You mean you are like that in other lessons too?' Questions, provided they are not simply rhetorical or abusive, make the kid become involved, and therefore to some extent exposed. One chat will not quell a crook for life, but it lets you glimpse the person behind the grinning face or piercing shriek that you cannot stand. More important, he knows that you have had that glimpse and may well want another. That prospect, without the defensive wall of friends' distraction and group power, may tone him down a bit. If it does not, the second chat may tell you more about him. Either way, if you can find the time to make it work it should help you, at the time and later.

A chat with a kid, however, although it may seem threatening and will be time-consuming, is not merely a disciplinary device. You may talk to a kid simply as a punishment, to make him feel vulnerable or to occupy his time, but you may also talk to him to reassure him, to ask about work problems, to explain what you are trying to do, to listen to a grievance, to ask for helpful suggestions or simply to find out more about him; and the real purpose of a chat may well alter as it proceeds. With this multiplicity of purpose you move, rightly, out of the mere technique of control and into the development of relationships. A series of chats, some within lessons, some enforced, some casual, will take you closer to kids so that you get to know them better, get used to the things that anger or irritate them, stop doing the things that will make them misbehave and get to know what might deter them from disruption. At that stage, although you are not clear of all discipline problems, you are beginning the work of real teaching, and it is at that threshold of discovery, peculiar to you and to your classes, that books on discipline become superfluous.

Chapter 9

Alone Together

The teacher is alone with his class. That may not be an ideal situation, and it may well change, but at the present moment, for most teachers in most schools, it remains true. The essential loneliness of the teacher in action is one of the factors which makes the first years of work so difficult, and it is because of that vulnerable isolation that I have tried to detail what the teacher can do to help himself. He may well receive valuable help from others, but he cannot rely solely on that possibility.

He is not, though, entirely alone. For he works in concert with other teachers, to whom he is bound by the common conditions of their work – they also are alone with their classes, who are the same children however differently they may behave. The teacher is thus not only responsible for his own temporary communities of the class-room, but is himself a member of the community of the staff-room, and that membership may require almost as much thought and care as his more obvious responsibility.

The significance of this dual loyalty may vary; some struggling teachers take refuge from hostile classes in a lively staff-room, while others may go to their lessons early to swap the programmed conversation of their colleagues for the refreshing sanity of kids. But whatever your personal situation, you need to be aware of other teachers in the same school, if only for the selfish, pragmatic reason that your relations with them may to some extent determine your own effectiveness. A staff-room should not be merely a chance for a breather, a pit stop wedged briefly into the Grand Prix of the time-table, but an instrument of discipline and a means to understanding. It is thus potentially a vital part of your resources and, like all equipment, it needs to be carefully examined before it will provide you with anything like satisfactory service.

Authority Structure and the Teacher

Formally, the young teacher starts work on the lower levels of a power pyramid, which at its worst may subject him to as petty and irritating

K

an attention as it inflicts on his kids. Some senior teachers persist in regarding younger colleagues as older pupils, to be talked to and allowed occasional responsibility or freedom, but hardly to be considered as equals. In extreme circumstances probationers can find themselves being told what to wear, how to speak and where to sit in the staff-room, as well as how to teach.

More frequent and serious problems are presented by the authority structure of the school in its dealings with pupils, particularly as regards the observation of school rules. The regular enforcement of these usually creates some difficulties, in the face of which the simplest course of action is to obey and apply every rule that the school contains, ignoring protests about what other teachers allow and trusting piously in the rewards of virtue. For anyone of any independence or intelligence, however, some schools make this course of action very difficult by retaining obscure and useless statutes for simply traditional reasons. Going it alone, on the other hand, although romantic and occasionally exciting, can lead to some painful dilemmas. In my own teaching I have taken some horrible risks which I would not dare contemplate now, and which I suspect were aimed rather at demonstrating my independence than at achieving anything worthwhile.

It must remain an individual decision, but the individual taking it must know that he is taking it. Farley, in *Secondary Modern Discipline*, suggests the following as 'The Teacher's Limits':

(1) No smoking or swearing *in your presence*.
(2) No conspiratorial arrangements to let individuals break school rules, however silly you may think they are.
(3) You expect a reasonable amount of work done in a presentable manner.
(4) You stick to the syllabus and the time-table (at least in spirit).
(5) No exchange of doubtful jokes.
(6) No criticism of other staff.
(7) No turning a blind eye to unpleasant incidents.
(8) No sarcastic remarks to pupils or unpleasant references to their species, mentality, etc.

I would not agree with all of these, but would accept much of the thinking behind them. Loyalty to colleagues is a delicate problem, especially when you know neither the kids nor the colleagues well. It is part of the teacher's responsibility to work out how what he does and says might be misinterpreted by kids, so that although you cannot guard against the wilder misunderstandings it is not sufficient to take refuge in mere 'honesty'. I would say that it is usually possible to avoid serious lying and professional betrayal, but in extreme situations it may call for a lot of care and tact.

As to breaking rules, I would do this if I seriously thought it necessary, but under the following conditions:

(1) I must have a good reason, for which I am prepared to argue.
(2) Ideally, the kids concerned should not be aware that a rule is being broken; *but*
(3) if the kids must know, I should take maximum steps to let them know why I am breaking the rule and within what limits; that is, I must not leave the impression that I will always ignore the rule I happen to be breaking.
(4) If senior members of staff find out any of what has happened, I should tell them as much as possible as soon as possible, and be prepared to discuss what I have done calmly. I may not be allowed to, but that breakdown must not be my fault.

Simply because they are arbitrarily composed, and people's consciences are various and tender, I think it is unrealistic to demand that all teachers must unreservedly commit themselves to applying all rules. But I do think that every teacher needs his own basic list of the things he will not tolerate – simply, those things which he will spend most time and energy discouraging, and which he will *never* simply ignore. It is important to compose such a list in the cold light of day, because crisis conditions develop with terrifying speed and paralyse the teacher's objectivity, so that it is often too late by the time you realise just what a kid has got away with. My own list of absolutes goes as follows:

(1) Open defiance or cool rudeness (which is not hysterical, wild).
(2) Blatant lying (e.g. when I have seen a kid do something which he then denies).
(3) Preventing other kids from being involved in the lesson (interrupting comments, jogging writing arms, kicking furniture, etc.).
(4) Causing serious damage to property.
(5) Vindictive bullying, whether physical or not.
(6) Another teacher in real trouble (only in cases of intolerable injustice would I refuse to help – if in doubt, preserve the communal façade, however transparent).
(7) Deliberate viciousness in myself, whether verbal or physical.

No one has to accept this list, or Farley's, or choose between the two. But I think it helps every teacher to make up his own and decide to stick to it. This at least gives some sense of foundation and continuity to the chaos of discipline questions, since when you recognise one of your absolutes looming up, at least one of your uncertainties is resolved; you may not know how to act, but you are sure that you must. Going down in flames is preferable to doing nothing in the face of x; x, of course, being whatever you choose in advance to make it.

Many would say that this is too individualist, leaving decisions to the private conscience which should be made for the school as a whole. As (6) above should indicate, I think it is important that discipline should be seen by both staff and kids as a corporate matter, and this obviously involves delicate discretion, especially where being rude about other staff might seem to offer an easy popularity. But although it is possible and essential to have a network of trust in which teachers rely on their colleagues not to undermine them personally, I do not think it is reasonable to expect detailed conformity of policy over a staff of eighty or more, unless they have been specifically appointed to serve in a certain type of school. The contexts of discipline in a large school are so various, and the personalities of the staff cover such a wide range, that uniformity is impossible. In my view, most kids accept this (provided that each teacher makes clear what he personally will and will not tolerate) and adapt to it with chameleon skill; indeed, the lesson in 'how adults behave' which we are constantly giving is one of the richest and most important sections of the large school's hidden curriculum.

Most sets of rules are drawn up by the Head or passed down like Mosaic tablets, and it is that distance from individual staff which make them difficult to enforce. It may be that we shall eventually develop saner sets of rules and wiser attitudes to their enforcement, but the democratisation of school rules (whether among staff, or between staff and pupils) is neither an instant nor a simple solution. Staff majorities may often insist on applying a rule which individual teachers regard as unimportant, and the more democratic the process of rule-making, the greater is the obligation on all staff to observe and enforce whatever has been agreed. Communal discipline requires of a teacher a loyalty to colleagues which is quite as binding (although it may often seem less appealing) as his loyalty to kids. Any fool can exercise solidarity with his friends, but to be loyal to another teacher with differing views can be a nastily delicate test.

The Staff-Room

To a nervous beginner, the first comprehensive staff-room can be terrifying. Large numbers of people, some of them moving purposefully across the room, others relaxing in friendly conversation, easy jokes and endless cups of tea, but all utterly at home with each other and the job they do. That at least is the impression, and many happy schools quite unintentionally depress newcomers by the loud, hurried assurance of their staff-room atmosphere.

The numbers, too, are bewildering. From your own school days you may have remembered a select group of begowned, middle-aged intellectuals, decorously concealed behind a thick wooden door on which you dared not knock. Here there are many groups, confined in a small space and buzzing busily. Talk is not dominated by one group of men discussing their carburettors, or ladies comparing knitting patterns, but the multiplicity of possible life-styles is at first confusing rather than cheering, even though in the long run a large staff is more likely to provide you with at least some kindred spirits. In the short term, find an ally as soon as possible; sex, age or status do not matter, but you need someone to whom you can put all those questions which might sound stupid in public. Nearly every school has its own peculiarities of operation, and it is rare for them to be adequately explained by the formal announcements.

The conditions and the size, however, are not half as frightening as the attitudes. Many probationers and students find the staff-room unnerving, because of the vehemence and frequency with which its members contradict all their dearest assumptions about teaching. This is a random sample from one school where I taught, and in many comprehensives both the sentiments and the language would be far worse:

'Keep the buggers down, that's all that matters.'
'I'm the boss in my class-room, and that's it. I'm sorry, but anyone who disagrees will find himself in trouble.'
'I love 'em – and I kick 'em to death.'
'I don't mind admitting I am a bit old-fashioned. I think we all are when it comes down to it.'

Students trained within a consensus which assumes belief in child-centred methods and humane approaches may find such talk disturbing, and all the more so for the assurance with which it is voiced. There is a toughly 'realistic' tone which implies that no sane listener would venture to disagree – 'I think we all are', says the 'old-fashioned' young teacher, and he would be genuinely surprised to find his confidence disputed.

The cynicism is nothing like as widespread or deep-rooted as it often appears. There are bitter teachers, just as there are lazy, perverted or sadistic teachers, but they are not a majority. Many of those who in conversation seem heartless are in action deeply committed to helping kids, and many genuinely progressive teachers do not debate their ideals in the staff-room, either because they know they will change nothing by mere discussion or because they have better things to do. Also, like social workers, doctors and priests, teachers can sometimes find relief from the intensity of involvement with their clients by satirising the process in which they are involved. For all these reasons, staff-room cynicism should not be taken as a reliable index to the dedication or actual attitudes of the teachers in that school. It is there, though, and needs looking at more closely.

Part of the cynicism is surely a reaction to the assumptions of educational theory; 'I don't mind admitting' and 'I'm sorry' in the above quotations both suggest mock-apology to an orthodoxy which will be offended. Schools, like prisons, do not always follow the principles outlined at the level of public discussion, and many teachers resent being expected to revere values and methods handed down from above, by people who may not be involved in the actual work of applying them. The safety valve for this frustration is the underground of casual discussion; the NFER, DES and TES can waffle on for ever, but they cannot touch you for what you say in the staff-room.

This also accounts for some hostility to research and experiment. In the excitement of discovery many researchers have treated schools as their private laboratories, disrupting classes and habits for just long enough to test a pet hypothesis, after which they have left the teachers and cleaners to pick up the rubbish. This growth industry attracts swarms of potential Piagets, armed with unlimited time, sheaves of paper and quite nauseating zeal. Some of them may eventually come up with valuable results, but it is not surprising if the teachers should occasionally yawn; they know who will be teaching their classes for the rest of the year.

Teachers are not, in fact, quite as indifferent to progress or innovation as their reactions might suggest. Within the school, most staff have time and genuine respect for colleagues who achieve something new and important, particularly where it obviously benefits the kids they teach. Confronted with such gains, within the conditions of work they share, many older staff show a capacity for sensitive appreciation and real change which would astonish their critics; what is resented is not innovation in itself, but talk about it from those who merely talk.

This harsh but understandable realism underlies the caution which also characterises staff-room conversation. To many probationers, older teachers seem paranoid about the threats of noise, damage or complaint, because these are the objections constantly raised to any new proposal. There is some unthinking conservatism, but even the limited concern for safety may have its roots in realism; not all teachers are capable of imaginative gestures or striking innovation, and their apparent cowardice may be shrewd self-knowledge, fortified by the necessary recognition that their work requires the steady rhythm of a five-day week rather than sporadic superb performances. Also, what you do can make it impossible for other people to do what they want to do; it is not fair to do drama immediately outside a maths lesson where a teacher is having trouble, or to lend out the music department record-player when they need it for the next lesson, but it is only through listening to other staff rehearse their moans that you realise the problems you may be causing. Generalisations about teachers are just as doubtful as generalisations about kids, but in so far as they are cautious it is often because of their past experience and their intimate knowledge of their working conditions. It is worth waiting until you have shared some of that experience and knowledge before you condemn their caution; they may not be quite as stupid as they look.

Conditions of work may account for teachers' caution, but they do not explain the full force of their cynicism, which can be ferocious. My own suggestion is that the worst cases are caused by a philosophical vacuum, a lack of intelligent purpose, which is best illustrated by a true anecdote, told to me by one of the participants.

Two teachers are spending a free lesson reading the papers and chatting when they hear a riot proceeding above them. They listen carefully, until they hear the strains of a teacher's voice, sometimes above the din but in no way controlling it. Having ascertained that the class has not simply been left unattended, they discuss intervention:

A: What do you think?
B: I'm supposed to be free. I only get four a week.
A: Me too.
B (Nodding in the direction of the head's office): Let him look after it – he is getting paid for it.
A: Yeah. Five thousand quids' worth.

They resume talking and reading the papers, while the din goes on, the teacher keeps shrieking and the head draws his £5,000 per annum until the bell provides a welcome respite for them all.

The 'philosophical vacuum' here is the total lack of direction in the teachers' conversation. Their early pause suggests that they knew something important was going on, but they did not seriously think about what the situation required. If the class had been left, both recognised a simple duty to supervise it, but since a teacher was present and technically responsible it was harder to make a polite and effective intervention. Either teacher could easily have contained the trouble, and both were good-natured enough to sympathise with a struggling colleague, but neither of these factors was enough to make them act; instead, they were guided by two utterly irrelevant considerations – money and status.

The concern with position and reward goes far deeper in teaching than any 'professional' code, and is almost entirely harmful. A bad situation is aggravated by the allocation of special allowances, which picks out certain teachers and raises them above their colleagues, thus encouraging showing-off, jealousy and tension. The winners become excited by success and plan more of it, the losers become bitter and leave extra work to their better-paid 'superiors', and the kids lose out. Extreme careerists lose sight of their pupils completely: their targets are a Scale 4 in two years, or a headship by Christmas, and they will do or say almost anything to secure that Holy Grail – including feigning progressive ideals, deserting classes in mid-course or stimulating extra-curricular activity for just long enough to fill in a *curriculum vitae* with a shred of honesty. Even below the 'high-fliers' after their headships, the image persists of pedagogic monkeys scrambling up a ladder whose rungs narrow as they get higher.

Most jobs have their careerists, and a few would not matter, but in education they are most widespread where there is least sense of purpose. If the school has an overall sense of direction, and provides intelligent aims and satisfying ways of working, teachers are happier in their work, put more into it and explore the possibilities of co-operation much further. If, on the other hand, the school lacks direction, distrusts its teachers and frustrates any initiatives they may promote, its members of staff are much more likely to become competitive individuals, working against each other to gain the status which will suggest they are doing something worthwhile.

Mathematical measurements, like wage levels, or scale posts, are ideal for such reassurance since they seem so definite. 'From basic to Scale 4 in three years' sounds so exact it must mean something, and that solid feeling of numerical progress may help you to forget that the first school was fun and the second a dreary factory.

For teachers unsure of their role, therefore, money and power can be signs of achievement, but so too can discipline. 'Jones can't cope' or 'If you can't control them, you will never do anything', have a tough, definite air of black-and-white precision, where you can either manage or you can't. 'Can you handle Harris?' becomes a test of virility, a way to sort out the teaching men from the boys. The men who feel they can manage, can cope, can handle so-and-so, will get reassurance from talking about it, reminiscing over old riots they have quelled, or tough nuts they have battered into submission. They may even occasionally joke over old failures, like the kid who refused to pick up his pen even after he had been slapped eight times, but generally the picture is one of fiercely amiable power.

Whatever its roots, such conversation is damaging both to the school as a whole and to the development of a young teacher's discipline. The words he hears may be depressing or deeply wounding – 'That history girl's having trouble, I see' or 'He'll have to sort 3B out quick or he has had it' – but they probably will not lead to any useful solution. The hard men have either forgotten or pretended to forget their own moments of insecurity, and although some of their talk is bluff, some of it really does reflect the way they think and teach; either way, they seem positively to discourage any serious consideration of the probationer's problems.

For in such an atmosphere it takes real nerve to admit failure. Specific discussions about what ought to happen to Kevin, who has just thrown a chisel at a teacher, may well be lively, specific and most informative; but the milder difficulties ('They just will not shut up') do not usually get aired, just because everyone else seems so assured. You dare not risk the certain exposure and probable contempt that such a confession would attract. Consequently, you keep your growing problems to yourself, try to hide all signs of dismay from your colleagues, and bluff along as cheerfully as you can, while the situation gets steadily worse.

This does not always happen, of course, and a lot of teachers are individually helpful and reassuring to young teachers in trouble. But where there is a dominant staff-room cynicism, and no honest discussion of the problems of control, life for the probationer is very tough. The easiest way out is often the worst, a sudden renunciation of all he has been taught and has tried to believe in, and a new authoritarianism only distinguished from the old cynics' by its convert's enthusiasm. Peter Newell, in his fervently abolitionist book on corporal punishment, describes this phenomenon with sad, wondering dismay: '. . . while the colleges of education may on the whole encourage a non-punitive approach, young teachers' first experience of schools and the influence of older colleagues very often bring out authoritarian attitudes.'[1]

This process needs looking at a lot more closely, and it is not sufficient merely to hint at 'the influence of older colleagues' as though they were industrial communists or professional pornographers. As with any corruption, the key factor is the person being corrupted; just where do these 'authoritarian attitudes' come from? Were they there all the time? In which case, why were they not explored during the period of training? Or have they been simply and suddenly instilled? If so, it suggests either that the non-punitive approach has been very superficially examined, or else that conditions in schools are so totally removed from the world of teacher-training that colleges are literally wasting their time.

The colleges, hopefully, would be able to pursue this inquiry with more rigour, but a key factor is surely the teacher's conditions of work. If many young staff do adopt the views of older colleagues, it is because they have the minimal assurance that those views match the job, that a person with that time-table, forced to make those decisions about those kids, can survive with this philosophy. Many probationers do not feel even that confident about the philosophy of teaching which they have been encouraged to express during training, and in crises it can be a comfort to follow someone who looks as though they know what they are doing, however unattractive they may seem in absolute terms. What young teachers and older teachers share is the knowledge that they are in the same boat; the destinations of many educationists may be far more appealing, but they are travelling by a different route.

The Young Teacher in the Staff-Room

You have, then, adjustments to make which are not directly related to your relationships with kids but will certainly affect them. Both your dealings with the pyramid of power and your place in the staff-room will affect how you feel about a particular school, and will probably restrict what you can do.

With both parties, I would advise caution, and again for practical reasons. In staff-room discussion, particularly, it is not always worth jumping in feet first the minute anyone says something with which you

---

[1] P. Newell, *A Last Resort?* (Penguin, 1972), p. 151.

violently disagree. Firstly, most teachers are not so recently accustomed as you are to fierce and friendly debate, and may well take a quick remark or angry interruption as sheer arrogance. Secondly, you are unlikely to persuade anyone by merely verbal argument; if you really want to shake up a stuffy staff-room, show them what adventurous teaching can achieve with the kids they teach, but do not shoot off your mouth until you are sure you have got something to talk about.

The power pyramid, too, is often unsympathetic, easily offended and difficult to persuade. In terms of power, you are almost helpless, so that unless you are lucky in having a sympathetic Head you are best off being left alone. If you are compelled to go against deep conviction, fight and then leave, but if the cause is trivial simply listen politely and go away. Silence under duress is not consent, and a Head out for your blood can make life very, very awkward.

Nicholas Otty, in *Learner Teacher*, provides a graphic illustration of the probationer's problems, and an unwitting object lesson in how not to treat other members of staff. He is understandably concerned with himself and his own reactions, as we all are, but this leads him into the assumption that he is in some way uniquely enlightened: '. . . there is the world of Peter Langland and Nigel Moore, on the edge of which are John and Allan and Philip, which borders all the time on delinquency. There are fights "up the youth clubs" and window-smashing and petty thefts. I wonder how aware the other teachers are of this.'[1]

With his own discipline, Otty runs into the same problems as the rest of us. A second-year class has 'declined rapidly' within three weeks of the beginning of term; 'to begin with they were quiet and wary, and they did as they were told. Three weeks later they do exactly as they want'.[2] He describes an encounter with Mr Daniels ('a good man . . . an experienced and successful teacher'), who has offered help.

'From the front of my head I hear a distant, calm, reasonable voice. It tells Mr Daniels things I like to think, and it has no connection with the deep centred panic in my mind.

' "That's very kind, Mr Daniels, but I would rather carry on on my own!"

' "Oh well, that's fine, as long as you feel you have a grip on them when you need it."

' "No, I have no 'grip on them', but then I don't want to have."

'His eyes shoot up spreading wrinkles towards his bald crown. "You

[1] N. Otty, *Learner Teacher* (Penguin, 1972), p. 99.
[2] Ibid., pp. 82–3.

see I don't want them to work for me because of *my* control. They must learn from their own control, the value of co-operation and the intrinsic value of what they are studying. . . ."

'Brave words, brave words. But he takes them – and he appears to be convinced.'

This is a classic example of probation schizophrenia, where the surface doctrine of progressive trust ('from the front of my head') collides with the primitive urges of power and self-preservation ('the deep centred panic in my mind'). It is a reflection on Otty's training that he has not been prepared for such a conflict, and some condemnation of the school that he does not feel free to admit the internal contradiction.

He does not help, though. He has not thought out what he is trying to do, and the irony of his tone effectively undermines any weight his patter ('things I like to think') might otherwise carry. To Mr Daniels he pretends indifference to any form of teacher control, but in private his own account of the lesson is much more honest about the realities of power and his own authoritarian wishes: '2B's behaviour has *declined* rapidly. . . . They do exactly as they want.' If the patter means anything at all, how can this be seen as 'decline'?

In many schools it would be necessary to hide the problems and disguise the mental confusion, but in this case Mr Daniels is sincerely offering help, tactfully and in private. It would be only courtesy to listen to what he might have to say, and if the advice is wholly inappropriate it could always be quietly ignored. By wheeling out his defensive, half-digested philosophy, however, Otty suggests that all is well, and thus cuts himself off from the help he seems likely to need.

In his dealings with the hierarchy he is similarly confident, and deprives himself of potential help in identical fashion. He has been holding a 'sex-before-marriage' discussion with a third-year class, and has been summoned to the Head's study:

' "It's too early in you, you, perhaps you lack the, it needs experience to tackle such a subject."

' "I didn't tackle it exactly. They brought it up and wanted to talk about it."

' "Well, subjects, I think it would be, subjects like this really come under my 'Education for Adult Life' course."

' "But they wanted to talk about it *now*, not the January after next. I do feel it is important, Mr Curle, to take these matters as they arise naturally for the children."

' "Oh, I quite agree, but it takes a lot of know-how to guide a discussion of that kind."

' "A guided discussion is not a discussion. I can't decide their conclusions before we start." '

Otty defends himself wittily, but the enjoyment of the debate with Mr Curle blinds him to possible criticisms of his own teaching. He says 'They brought it up', implicitly disclaiming responsibility for the choice of subject matter, but his own account of the lesson reveals that a small group, and two boys in particular, did the actual demand-ing, and that Otty agreed to it as a kind of dare. He did not, apparently, take a vote about other possible topics, or even ask for suggestions. Did he not know that sex is a classic 'sniffing out' topic for new teachers?

Mr Curle tells him that 'it takes a lot of know-how to guide a dis-cussion of that kind', and even if he is 95 and a lifelong Methodist, he is right. Otty insists on equating 'guided' with 'indoctrinated' and so misses the point. With a class discussion, particularly when it in-volves thirty 13-year-olds and an interesting topic, the teacher is responsible for certain things: ensuring everyone has the chance to speak; enabling listeners to hear muffled or embarrassed contributions; providing any necessary information; ensuring that the discussion is serving all the members of the group; and relating what is said to other work in school, and the life of each kid outside. That is what I mean by guiding a discussion, and it has got no connection with telling kids what to think. I do not know if it is what Mr Curle meant, but Otty's combative attitude did not give him the chance to explain.

One thing Otty might have 'guided' was Peter, who apparently 'kept very aloof, occasionally throwing in some appallingly crude remark about "scrubbers" or "virgins" '.[1] Otty records that, but does not say if he did anything about it; the implication is that he would have felt it to be a defeat for him to suggest to Peter that he had been shocking, so that he calmly ignored the provocation. What it does not suggest is what thinking Otty did about the other kids in the class, their likely reaction to such comments and the interests of their parents, to whom he is responsible. That whole area is of course complex, and difficult to bear in mind if you are excited with your own teaching, but it is precisely for that reason that you need to discuss what you are doing with people who have taught a bit longer and who continually have to remember their wider responsibilities – like headmasters, for instance. Mr Curle might have been a wise old

[1] Ibid., p. 87.

teacher or a stuffy old fool, but Otty might have done himself some good if he had assumed the first rather than the second.

It is not easy to ask for help, and in power situations we all tend to react like kids – keep the authority at bay, fight back if you can, but at any rate get it all over as fast as possible. Those are the dictates of self-preservation, and some Heads still make them necessary. Where possible, though, however naked it makes you feel, it is worth trying to look at the situations in which you are so powerfully involved, and to see them through the eyes of others – including staff who have been through similar situations and recovered from similar mistakes to yours. This means discussion, and honest discussion with people who are prepared to recount in realistic detail their own successes and failures.

To such discussion staff cynicism acts as a serious barrier, but so too does youthful arrogance. If young teachers enter the staff-room giving the impression that they have been divinely chosen to show this decrepit collection of fuddy-duddies how to do their job, it is not entirely surprising that no one rushes to help after their sandcastles have collapsed.

From my own experience I would say that such dialogue between young and old, as well as between grammar and sec.mod., graduate and non-graduate, academic and technical, is possible, mutually valuable and far too rarely attempted. It requires patience and restraint on both sides, and produces gradual gains which are sometimes barely visible. Some teachers may feel most secure alone and uncomfortable *en masse*, but from the point of view of the kids, as well as of their individual discipline, they work best when they are prepared to share communally the secrets of their isolated role; they are alone together.

PART THREE: SOLUTIONS

Chapter 10

Efficiency and Care

Part Two of this book has presupposed a largely individual warfare, with an isolated young teacher seeking to establish control over his class. This account slanders the large number of experienced teachers who do work hard and successfully at integrating new teachers into their schools, but my aim has been to arm students against the worst rather than to describe the average.

Even the average, however, is a long way from perfect, and most teachers of any sensitivity and imagination would want to improve the basis of their relationship with their pupils, so as to minimise those elements which feel most destructive, narrow-minded and petty. This change can be effected, but it is not anything like so simple and swift a job as some non-teachers imagine, and it does have to be done systematically rather than individually. The purpose of the present chapter will be to explore those organisational changes which would in my view best alter the context of teacher-pupil relationships, and thus make the kind of tactical struggle envisaged in the previous chapters both less bitter and less likely.

Training

To begin with, most TTIs need very much closer links with the schools to which they send their students. Many of these schools may well be reactionary, disorganised or hostile, but nothing can excuse the deliberate training of young teachers for an educational world which does not yet exist – and may never exist. Far too many lecturers use their students as guinea pigs, missionaries or cannon fodder, and nearly all fail to prepare them for the coming stresses and crises of class management.

Generally, the TTIs need closer co-operation with schools, which means a much more fluid and regular interchange of staff, more detailed consultation on the deployment and precise use of students and far less preoccupation with the ideal teaching situation. More specifically, a small amount of time could deliberately be allocated to the study of discipline, through at least some of the following means: group discussion of simulated crisis situations (drawn from books, films or real life; or, like 'Out of Control', specially contrived); analysis of a detailed initial programme for teaching a difficult class (like Chapter 7, with details of subject material added); group and individual assignments on the practical and ethical problems of controlling kids (In what way is the teacher 'other'?; A difficult kid and the class as a whole; the limits of the teacher's power; why punish? How to punish, in a series of hypothetical situations; and so on). For those interested in pursuing a more academic line, Keith Wadd's essay on 'Classroom Power' (reprinted in *Discipline in Schools* (Ward Lock, 1973)) offers a promising starting-point, if there are education lecturers prepared to follow it.

In many cases, such attention would involve a change not only in teaching content but in method. The child-centred gospel is still transmitted by far too many lecturers through teacher-centred means, and the subjective nature of discipline precludes such authoritative treatment. For students to be fully involved, their intentions and fears to be honestly faced, TTIs will have to create an atmosphere of genuine discussion, in which prejudices are aired, doubts raised, and contrary views related and explored; the achievement of such an atmosphere, indeed, will be more important than the conclusions reached or the academic respectability of the views expressed. This will demand a more trusting and flexible maturity than many TTIs are used to, since the aim will be, not to maximise the number of converts to any given creed, but to make as many teachers as possible as fully conscious as possible of the implications of their own attitudes.

Restructuring the Schools

In contemplating large-scale changes in schools, as in analysing an individual breakdown of class control, it is vital to be specific. To 'tighten up all round', 'heighten the tone' or 'reverse the swing of the pendulum' are meaningless exercises, since these general myths suggest no particular action. To be effective, we have to plan clearly what we are doing, decide what we are after and identify the abuses we seek to guard against or cure – for instance truancy, noise, vandalism, disobedience or smoking in the lavatories. Not all school problems can be simply defined or solved, but the attempt at precision has nonetheless to be made.

In outlining my personal suggestions for the running of an effective comprehensive school, I have in mind the following problems, which currently represent a potential threat to the smooth running of many schools:

Teachers: the isolation of most class teachers; the ineffectiveness of teachers, some of us most of the time and most of us some of the time; the discontinuity brought about by absence or staff turnover; and the inevitable discrepancies of treatment and divergences of opinion between different members of a large staff.

Parents: the ignorance of many parents about modern education, and in some cases their suspicion, or outright hostility, towards it; more particularly, the uncertainties of those who view comprehensive schools as a new and frightening phenomenon; also, the chilling indifference of a small group of parents towards their children's education.

Pupils: the sheer range of possible behaviour, including:
    (1) day-to-day routine (equipment, movement about school, punctuality, attendance);
    (2) relationships with teachers (disobedience, cheek);
    (3) social development (ranging from the difficult borderline areas of chewing gum, swearing and smoking to the more flagrant violations of bullying, vandalism and theft);
    (4) exceptional incidents (unpredictable, irregular and extreme).

Within the space available it would be silly to try and offer a total blueprint, adequate for every situation. Also, the outline which follows, although a personal, highly subjective sketch, draws heavily on the work of existing schools and makes no great claims to originality. It may nonetheless be useful as a framework for discussion, and does indicate one of the directions in which schools might develop in order to free themselves from some of their present tensions and difficulties.

Teachers

We urgently need to mobilise the teacher resources already at the schools' disposal. Far too many staffs are paralysed by a hierarchical system which assumes that initiative, effort and disciplinary responsibility are as severely rationed as salary points, and allocated to the same personnel. A more democratic arrangement, allowing teachers a greater say in how they should best operate, would not only improve the atmosphere of the school but make it more efficient, since most people work better and harder for causes they have helped to define.

Within houses and departments, this would mean a more equal sharing of information and decisions, as well as of equipment, materials and classes. It would also involve a wider spread of disciplinary functions, so that the experience, skill and time of all members would become available to all other members. Staff in trouble could be helped by the timely arrival of colleagues 'popping in to pick up a book', experienced teachers would brighten their lessons by selective borrowing from younger and possibly brighter minds, and nervous innovators might well find the confidence to try out their schemes in the company of old hands less adventurous in their thinking but more secure in their control. Whether or not this is formalised into 'team teaching', such an approach would gradually extend the talents and experience of individual teachers, and the possibilities for the whole school.

In the short term, every department would have its own network for dealing with petty offenders. Being late for lessons, not bringing equipment, forgetting to do homework, and so on, all cause some teachers anxiety and would need to be dealt with before they became raging epidemics. The department would therefore ensure (*a*) that common expectations on these matters were agreed, and made clear to all kids, and (*b*) that other members of the department were available if necessary. This need not be a hierarchical process; there is no reason why a forgetful adolescent should be impressed by a 'head of department' title, and in many cases he might not be the best person for this particular job. It can even be rotated; one highly efficient 'hatchet man' I knew used to deal with everybody's errant pupils but his own, whom he referred to a willing colleague. All that is needed is another voice and face, to remind the kid (away from the distraction of his mates and the surrounding lesson) that certain things are necessary. If this reminder is ignored, the convenient stranger might have to resort to some trivial punishment (like reporting regularly with books previously forgotten, or having to turn up five minutes early to a lesson for which the culprit was late). Often, the mere presence of another adult would be sufficient. Persistent thoughtlessness and lateness are usually gestures of deliberate casualness, to test out or provoke an individual teacher. In this case, the kid would be confronted with a system as well as a person; if he or she can work with the person, well and good, but at a certain point of defiance, the system takes over. If you do x, then y will happen. This is not a permanent scheme of oppression; once established, it should not have to be frequently used, and individual teachers might well prefer to opt out of it entirely. The point is that it should be there, an existing neutral aid for teachers facing personal battles, and not a sullen, short-term dramatic rescue, hastily improvised and soon forgotten.

This need not be impersonal in a restrictive sense. Such a system would be intended to minimise lesson distraction, so as to enable the personal talents of both teacher and taught to flourish. 'Personality' has its limits, and even the most dynamic peddlers of charisma get ill, go on courses or leave, so that each school needs to *depend* on personal gifts as little as possible. In an effective school, additional talents, interests and sacrifices would of course be welcome, but for day-to-day running (administration, teaching materials and petty discipline) we need intelligent, practical systems.

None of this would work if it were simply announced as law. Teachers have not generally been accustomed to being consulted about what they do; in some cases, indeed, they have been positively discouraged from thinking about it, and have become attached to the undemanding torpor of blind obedience. In seeking to give staff a more vital, interesting and active role, therefore, a school would also have to provide them with regular opportunities to discuss their work, problems and immediate needs.

Most of such discussion would need to take place between small groups with similar interests and experiences, in houses and departments, in an honest atmosphere where confessions and complaints could be aired without fear of subsequent retaliation. The school's demands and expectations of its pupils would be discussed by those most intimately connected with presenting them, and senior teachers would be brought up far more forcibly than usual against the classroom consequences of their decisions.

In fact, such a system would give senior teachers more importance rather than less. Instead of simply sitting astride a pyramid over which their qualifications and experience have won them domination, they would have steadily to work for an atmosphere in which their members of staff were both more independent and better supported than before. This would be a delicate long-term task, whose goal – like that of all good teaching – would be eventual self-elimination; the good head of department is one whose departure is not disastrous.

An established habit of honest talk, spread through interlocking houses and departments, must make teachers more aware of their own intentions and of the school's needs. Their analyses and remedies would not always agree, and some decisions would still be made autocratically, but it would be clear which decisions those were, and critics would at least be able to air their opposition. Differences would be acknowledged more openly, and much of the stifled aridity of staff-room sniping would evaporate. Practically, there would be more chance of intervention by staff in those thousand and one trivial incidents which are no one's clear responsibility and which determine the disciplinary climate of a school, and in the course of that intervention staff would have a greater sense of moral and actual support for having previously discussed similar cases with their colleagues.

Parents

This extended atmosphere of discussion should also include parents, in a variety of ways. At the moment 'getting the parents in' is simultaneously the ultimate sanction and a signal of surrender, the dreaded confession that the school has failed. If we made a point of seeing more parents more regularly, we might well have fewer such crises. For example, it is quite possible for parents to see tutors about their children's subject options, to talk about progress reports as well as to get them through the post, to visit school departments to see – or even attempt – the work their children do, and to attend and participate in open meetings and small group discussions with members of staff about matters of mutual interest.

Those schools which make and maintain such contacts handle their kids better, simply because they know so much more about them. Also, they have a faster and more accurate indication of when something is going wrong. A visit to a parent is not the invariable solution to all discipline problems, and it is common experience to visit a child's home angry and to come out empty-handed in terms of power but far more sympathetic towards the child. That visit is nonetheless important, as a sign of attention and care which, though often incalculable, is always worthwhile.

Pupils

It is, of course, the kids that matter, and it is the arrangements most directly affecting them which are crucial. My effective school would therefore maintain a pastoral network which ensured that each child in the school had one adult centrally responsible for his welfare. This tutor would have a group of about twenty-five such clients within his tutor group, and would only be able to spend time and energy on their interests because he would have the confidence that elsewhere in the school other teachers were acting as tutors for the whole pupil population.

Tutors would be grouped into houses together with their tutor groups, with heads of house responsible for overseeing their tutorial work, for dealing with emergencies and for relating events, problems and children within one house to the rest of the school. The post of head of house would thus be vital, to be carried out in school time by a teacher of imagination and energy, rather than to be offered as a consolation prize for those unlucky enough not to become heads of department but humble enough to inspect lavatories and hold assemblies.

The individual tutor within this system would thus have the reassurance that it was taken seriously, a valuation reflected in the priceless school currency of scale posts and teacher-time. The actual content of his work as a tutor might seem strange, and viewed in terms of each daily contribution trivial, but over the school year as a whole the system would benefit subject teachers and pupils alike, with probationary teachers probably gaining more than most.

At first, the tutor might be merely a provider of information or disciplinarian, passing on school notices or complaints from teachers about the behaviour of individuals within the tutor group. As both group and tutor became more confident, so he would receive more from them – complaints, suggestions for activities or requests for changes in lessons or the running of the school. From day to day his function would vary, as it would from pupil to pupil, but his overall aim would be to piece together for each child the various facets of his or her school life, both for recording purposes (reports, or parents' evenings, for example) and as a precaution in the event of any serious disturbance. Not all teachers find it easy to be sympathetic and efficient tutors, and most pupils would probably have other teachers whose company they would prefer, but this would not be intended as a spontaneous, ideal friendship. It would be a system, ensuring as a minimum that for each child there would be one adult in the school whose business it would be to know about his or her progress, achievements and difficulties.

For the control of individual children, a tutor might not always be instantly effective, any more than a subject teacher would be, but his mere existence would provide a target for information, suggestions and complaints. Class teachers driven to distraction or seeking more profitable approaches would contact the child's tutor, who would thus become the focus of varied insights over the whole range of school activity. Has Jane suddenly 'gone off'? Is she always like this with male teachers? Has anything happened recently to upset her? Which of her teachers got on with her last year? In each case, the tutor should have something to offer, and although he may not always be the right person to deal with a particular problem, he should know who that right person is.

I once had a very lively, strong-willed girl in my tutor group for three years. When I started at the school she was 12 and intensely difficult, capable of defying teachers, disrupting classes and generally causing havoc. When I left she was 15 and pretty much the same. I did not have a magic wand I could wave when she was about to cause trouble, but I did learn some of the danger signs and teaching errors which might spark her off. I saw a lot of her, frequently had visits from her during lunchtime if I was working in my room, and spent a lot of time talking to her. By the end of three years she knew that I was genuinely interested in her and in what she was doing, that I would stand up for her if I felt she had been unfairly treated and that I would ask her side of the story on the frequent occasions when I received a complaint. There was never any instantly effective sanction, but she did know that if she had got herself in serious trouble I would find out about it and talk to her about it, and that if she was blatantly rude during my inquiries I would pass her on to my head of house, who also liked her but was much better at sounding severe. (A carefully measured Mutt and Jeff act, this, which worked quite well.) I think that over the years she became more aware of her impact on other people and the effect of this on her own life, although she was obviously maturing in her own right at the same time and her progress under a different system could only be hypothetically estimated. I could not offer any teacher 'the answer' to Mary, but I could warn them not to nag her, tell them something about her background, explain what she was good at and what she liked, and offer the consolation that nobody else knew what to do with her either.

A relationship as calculated as this may seem cold to those who work impulsively. As it happens, I liked this girl (as well as being exhausted and exasperated by her), but even if I had not I would have had to do something for her. Such artificiality is an intrinsic part of a teacher's job; we have these kids in school and it is our professional responsibility to know how they are behaving as well as how much they are learning. The tutorial system might seem like an intensive spy network, but it is meant to work in the kids' interests, and it usually does. Establishing it as an effective system for the whole school would certainly be a lot better than leaving things to chance.

The tutorial network, though central and vital, is not sufficient. It indicates very practically to the kids that their individual welfare matters, but the time they spend physically in tutor groups will be no more than half an hour a day, and there are other messages we also need to transmit.

To begin with, my hypothetical school would need to minimise the considerable tensions among children which traditional procedures have always created and intensified. Our past obsessive concern with selection, not only at 11+ but within the grammar and secondary modern schools as well, has always labelled large numbers of kids 'not selected'. It is from such children, who know clearly if inarticulately that the school thinks little of them and cares less, that a large amount of 'trouble' has come in the past, although the main responsibility for that disruption does not lie with the children.

Schools should either abolish streaming, or question with far more rigour the selection procedures they currently take for granted. Where it is impossible to avoid some selection, there should be a determined effort to ensure that low streams receive at least equal treatment in terms of books, resources, trips, films and teachers. Indeed, so far as discipline is concerned, there is a strong case for allocating the most gifted, imaginative or experienced teachers to the bottom streams first, instead of the more popular reverse process.

Within subjects, teachers would seek to provide the opportunity for intelligent choice, giving all kids some chance of choosing what they intend to learn. This would not only reduce the friction generated by compelling bored kids to follow courses they regard as useless, but would also increase the kids' responsibility for their own work situation. A silly choice, or the inability to think ahead realistically, and they penalise themselves; a moment's thought, or an intelligent selection from alternatives, and they have made one more step away from dependence on teacher initiative, towards self-direction and the maturity which is the only basis for intelligent, social behaviour.

This is and must be a long process, carefully learned in stages through a series of carefully prepared choices; it cannot be proved or disproved on a make-or-break trial which offers one choice and withholds others if the wrong alternative has been chosen. This would take time and trust, and would be particularly wearing for teachers with children who have been used to other patterns; the sudden glimpse of freedom can be dangerous as well as exciting to those who have never been free. It is for this reason that the extension of choice, and growth of independence, should be part of a whole school's planned development, rather than the gambit of an individual teacher. Whatever your personal inclinations or talents, the extension of free choice to pupils in a school can only be real for them if that extension is being made in a number of areas, simultaneously and deliberately.

Within that overall movement there might well be a meaner, less attractive attention to detail which might seem to contradict the general development towards self-direction. However, checks on books and equipment, or attention to internal truancy and reasons for lateness, are not denials of pupil freedom but a sign of teacher interest. We can be indifferent to the loss of stock only if our supplies are unlimited or we are not interested in next year's intake; since neither of these would be true, efficiency would be rated quite as highly as care. In the long run, in fact, these two apparently contrasted values are not only compatible but positively interdependent. There just is no way to care for large numbers of people without being efficient. As soon as we become concerned for more than a chosen few, we are thereby committed to preparing, planning and taking overall views as well as to the more emotive and satisfying process of face-to-face contact. Pensions, Christmas cards, weddings and Oxfam all depend on efficient operation, and it would be remarkable if comprehensive schools were to be any different.

Given an active, caring and efficient staff, a school can solve most of its trivial problems most of the time. Epidemics of lateness, litter or silliness may flare up, but need not be decisive. Less crucial, too, will be the difficulties raised by seriously disturbed children, both in the impact they make upon the class-room atmosphere and in the unease or resentment that their treatment might provoke. Outstanding cases of uncontrolled behaviour have always given rise to serious anxiety and dramatic headlines, but if the overall atmosphere of the school is right, such cases need only be tragic for the individual involved.

He remains, however, and my future school would have to cope with him just as many current schools must try to. Brutal severity and lenient apathy are equally useless, the understandably weary responses of school authorities deprived of the time and personnel to do justice to difficult cases. If these are to be withdrawn (so as to allow normal lessons to continue), the children responsible must be withdrawn *to* something as well as *from* their class, and that something must be prepared and available, rather than a furtive improvisation under pressure. It must also not be so easy or attractive an alternative that more orthodox pupils feel cheated. Seriously disturbed pupils may well need some form of temporary sanctuary where they can be sure of closer attention and less pressure, but the attention will also have to be sufficiently close to detect sheer laziness or a passing need for a change of air. Whether staff are freed to run such a system, or are flexibly distributed around the time-table so as to provide extra staffing for critical lessons, it may well be that one of the fixed assumptions of teachers has to go – either the pattern of 1 : 30 teaching, or the certainty of a number of free lessons.

Given some such flexibility, a school can free staff to cope with emergencies (staff absence, a riot or a highly disturbed child) as well as to maintain contacts (with parents, other staff and other schools) and systems from which all staff will ultimately benefit. Many harassed teachers might well reject any idea of adding to the pressures already building up on them, but there is no question that if we seek to radically improve our teaching situation, we are forced to question arrangements and assumptions which have always seemed to be integral features of our work. If we continue to regard them as permanent, it may be that we shall be forced to go through the rigours of class-room warfare for some time to come.

Once we accept that it need not be wasteful for a teacher to be free in order to help other teachers, that we do not always need pupils in boxes of thirty with one teacher per box, that some pastoral needs are as urgent as some academic needs, then it immediately becomes possible to make more rational use of the teaching force. It also makes the need for more teachers clearer and more urgent than ever before.

Sadly, we lose large numbers of good, experienced teachers every year; they go out to pasture in teacher-training colleges and departments of education, and only the very bravest make the return trip. If pay structures and professional expectations could be adapted to a circular rather than linear pattern, we might have more lecturers and headmasters returning to be useful in the class-room. Unfortunately, while pay and promotion compress all energy into a narrowing, vertical scramble away from contact with kids, we shall continue to lose precisely those people most capable, not only of organising class-rooms, but also of actively helping others to learn that subtle and difficult art.

More generally, while levels of pay, gloomy publicity and LEA quotas restrict the freedom of schools to employ as many staff as they need, we can hope for little visible improvement. Even on the crude grounds of 'more control', an increase in the number of teachers would be justified. More imaginatively, more teachers now might accelerate an efficient, democratic restructuring of schools, which would in turn make teaching a more immediately enjoyable and exciting job, so attracting more and better recruits. Unfortunately, no merely rational pressure will change the situation. No single decision

M

could so transform the potential quality of our education as an increase in the number of teachers available, but we shall not see that decision made until teachers and parents develop the force to make an unassailable, logical argument politically effective.

Underlying this whole chapter has been the central assumption that we can change the quality of school life through careful organisation and rational thought. Educational thinking has for far too long been preoccupied with the teacher as hero, the personality whose human qualities are the solution to all problems. There will always be room for talented and imaginative individuals, but effort, teamwork and attention to detail are all quite as important as dynamism and decisive leadership. We need urgently to escape from the pursuit of supermen, since this vain search distracts us from the necessary task of making the most fruitful and practical use of the resources we already have. The changes outlined in this chapter, many of them taken for granted in a number of schools, do not depend on a new generation of geniuses or an annual injection of saints. This kind of school can be run, in England, now, with the teachers currently at work and in training. Some teachers and some areas might find such changes easier to effect than others, but all can move to some extent in this direction; that would, in my view, serve them better than attending to some of the more spectacular but less realistic 'solutions' currently on offer.

Chapter 11

Beyond Control

The Wrong End

A publisher said of this book:

'I am rather uneasy about taking a book which uses discipline as its main theme. This seems to me to be starting from the wrong end, as it were, since the problem is so closely woven into such matters as the structure of the school, teacher-child relationships, the compulsory nature of education, etc. . . .'

This is a widely accepted educational orthodoxy to which this book is diametrically opposed. To talk about discipline may well be to start 'at the wrong end' intellectually, but it is there precisely that the young teacher starts, with precious little help from those travelling by academically acceptable routes. Writing a whole book about discipline need not imply that it is all-important but it is primary in sequence if not in significance; problems of control may not be profound or lasting, but they are the first that the probationary teacher meets.

In the early months of a teaching career many probationers experience a crude collision between ideal prescription and actual possibility, placing them in a dilemma to which there is no solution short of compromise. You cannot do what you would like to do, and you do not like many of the things you seem forced to do. You could hardly be further from the archetypal situation of the philosopher – a solitary thinker formulating concepts, prescribing values and assessing alternative modes of conduct. Yet the young teacher in difficulties faces intellectual as well as practical problems, and there is no escape in unthinking action for its own sake; you will need every scrap of intelligence you can summon if you are to convert potential crisis into a fruitful teaching situation.

The crucial thinking, though, has to be done in parallel with the teaching, so that theory and practice interact daily, each informed by the findings of the other. Your teaching benefits from careful realistic analysis, just as your criteria and goals are clarified by the experience of particular success and failure. Such a process, fluid, tiring and subject to constantly changing circumstances, inevitably forces you into compromises (dictated by shortage of time, personal limitations and the cussedness of kids or colleagues). Some compromises are better than others, and we each have to work to find our own, but the aim must be a workable pattern of life rather than a pure, unassailable intellectual stance.

It is within that context that the insoluble questions arise, forcing desirable values into collision and compelling the teacher to make some decision, however unattractive. At what point do you refer a kid to another teacher? Are any children ineducable? When do you openly disagree with another member of staff? Are you ever going to hit a pupil and, if so, under what circumstances? Should rules be made if they cannot be enforced? Should punishment be carried out if it has no effect? In what conditions is it wrong for a teacher to have control? It is impossible to have ready, abstract answers to such conundrums, but you need nonetheless some notion of the difficulties which may arise.

The anxious novice with systematic tendencies may even like to construct his own basic philosophy of control, beginning from the elemental definitions:

What is a school crime? (violation of rules, something disapproved of, dangerous behaviour, something you do not like)

How is its seriousness to be measured? (effect on work, the culprit, other kids, the teacher, the school as a whole)

What motivates the crime? (silliness, 'sniffing out', fundamental need, social deprivation, the school régime)

What is the purpose of punishment? (retribution, deterrence, reform)

How is its severity to be measured? (motive of crime, its effect on others, its significance within the culprit's life)

The answers to such questions are, rightly, further questions, but they lead the inquirer into a more specific and detailed study of the ethics of pupil and teacher behaviour. The result may not be an impeccable system, but it will be a lot better informed and more practically useful than the abstractions which emerge from polarised debate.

Discipline for What?

Whatever our philosophical talents or leanings, all teachers need to do some basic thinking on what discipline is for, if only because the justifications in widest circulation are seriously inadequate. Chapter 2, for instance, demonstrated the dangers of applying a general world-view to the educational field, and the reactionary demand for discipline as an antidote to permissiveness, moral decay or political anarchy is unhelpful, since that vague prescription offers no clue as to the nature or extent of the discipline required. Such prophets deal in symbolic movement ('Has the Pendulum Swung Too Far?' asks Mrs Rowan's second chapter) rather than in particular measures or relationships.

In the same way, to suggest that we should control kids in a certain way simply because we were so controlled by our teachers is a lazy form of conservatism, which fails to take into account the varied substantial changes in behaviour and attitudes over the past thirty years, blandly assumes widespread satisfaction with the present system, and offers no positive guidelines for the future.

The spiritual approach, that children need to recognise something other than themselves, some limit to their own self-seeking, makes a valuable point but provides no relevant argument. The accidents of friendship and family life already teach this very practical lesson to all children at some time, and few of them will recognise the implausible equation of teacher with 'other things in life apart from me'. Teachers, in fact, are as much in need of cosmic humility as children, and the argument that discipline in schools rests on a universal need to have one's freedom of action curbed might easily backfire; by such reasoning, dictatorial headmasters and insensitive local authorities are good for the soul.

Psychological justifications for discipline are similarly vague, asserting that requisite virtues (independence, loyalty, obedience, consideration for others, respect for superiors, or even religious faith) follow from a type of control, without being very clear exactly how or why this happens. If our right to command children depends on the healthy effect such discipline has on their personalities, we need a lot more evidence about the impact we currently have on our customers. What about those children who patently have not responded to treatment – do they need more of the same, or a different treatment? Are those virtues which schools claim to have inculcated in the past really a product of schooling, or were they produced by a more complex social interaction? Do those who claim to have such virtues know where they got them from? Are they so sure, in fact, that they are virtues at all? (It is easy, for instance, to exaggerate the value of obedience as a quality in itself). This line of argument is inevitably subjective, and for that reason makes a weak and unsettling basis for the teacher's authority.

A utilitarian approach, popular with many parents as well as with some teachers, is that children must learn to do as they are told because that will be required of them when they start work; defying a teacher may not matter, but defying an employer or supervisor might mean the sack. This is a crude and clumsy line, subordinating education to work more brutally than most teachers would want to, and overlooking the practical truth that all children learn very fast if the point of the lesson is clear; a boy who has been persistently rude and lazy at school may well change in a week if he wants to keep the job which requires such a transformation of him. Also, although most of our pupils end up in some sort of work, it is not that easy to generalise about the nature of the power structure in which they will eventually find themselves; if we are to train kids for relationship with their future bosses, how do we teach a future stockbroker, farm-labourer, self-employed window cleaner or shop steward?

Our justification for control has to be far more closely related to the work and life of schools, since that may well be the only thing which all our pupils have in common. Discipline should thus be seen as enabling, a crude but necessary means to a variety of teaching ends. These cannot all be easily defined, but they include the satisfactory completion of school work, intellectual development, the growth of social maturity and confidence, and the avoidance of damage and injury. These ends also apply to all pupils, so that a further negative end is the avoidance of situations by which the interests of one child override those of another.

The traditional work situation is easy. Time has been allocated for purposeful activities, and children ought therefore to use it, which means that they should be neither absent, late nor idle. Teachers have some expertise, and therefore must have the power to initiate work, establish relevant working conditions and command attention. Without such power, they are unable to do the job demanded of them by society and implied by their position as teachers, so that they must find some means to achieve or regain such power. This is the task of discipline.

So far the theory, if not the practice, is straightforward. But there are shadowy areas where it is harder to be confident about means and ends, but where some kind of order is either helpful or essential. What kind of discipline, for example, is appropriate to a school camp, or a fire alarm, a disco or the last day of term? By what criteria does a teacher act when he discovers a class left unattended, or a fight in the playground during break?

Teaching continually throws up situations which are exceptional and unpredictable, but for which some action is essential. Many teachers consequently play safe on the basis of 'If in doubt, say no', which is always unattractive, and can harden into a perverse cultivation of obstinacy for its own sake, but is not an entirely stupid response since it allows the teacher at least a crude sense of consistency.

If the ideal is specific, rational justification, relating each assertion of authority to some clearly desirable consequence, the young teacher is in the worst position of all, since he cannot know in advance which consequences he will eventually desire. He may want everyone quiet, or sitting down, or handing in their books one at a time, but he may not know that he wants these things until a moment of crisis, by which time it will be too late to either explain or train his charges into the required pattern of behaviour. It is for this reason that Chapter 7 urges a number of measures which might not seem rational at the time but which may well seem so in retrospect.

Just as the probationer may well have to say and do some things he finds it hard to justify, so he may well have to take decisions which cannnot – should not, even – be justified to the kids they affect. He may also be cheated of the chance to explain himself later, since many kids who will argue passionately at the moment of a decision are neither equipped for nor interested in subsequent philosophical disputation. What matters in such a situation is not that all the kids should be happy all the time, but that the teacher should be as clear and honest with himself as possible. The mere fact that you are worried about the justice of what you do is a far better moral and intellectual safeguard than the volatile reactions of thirty adolescents; if in serious doubt, seek out a wise and sympathetic colleague in private, and ask for a straight opinion.

Reason, Justice and Freedom

For the individual teacher, 'What entitles me to impose my will over these children?' may well be the key philosophical question. It is also a general problem, however, to which a more organised attention might be directed. If we are going to pay people to practise the philosophy of education, reward and promote those teachers who study it in their spare time and compel students to attend lectures in it, we can surely ask for some consideration in that area to be given to a pressing educational problem.

Outside the sanctity of the four gospels, too, there are relevant areas of research on which lecturers, teachers and students could all be profitably employed. Case studies of individual kids, classes and teachers, or detailed analyses of discipline crises (involving comment from parents, staff and a variety of kids involved, as well as information on the social and individual backgrounds of the key participants), might not be easy to carry out in a scrupulous and responsible manner, but would certainly be valuable for students.

Conceptually, it would help if someone could refine the cruder categories of inquiry currently in use – the authoritarian and democratic teacher, for instance, or the middle-class and working-class family. The actual variations in viewpoint and behaviour are much subtler and more interesting than these caricatures imply, and both teacher attitudes and discipline in the home offer exciting opportunities for exploration.

Given the backing of some such communal effort at understanding, teachers in schools might be able to create an atmosphere in which the exercise of power was less arbitrary, more rational and of diminishing importance. It might not always be possible to justify ourselves in the heat of crisis to a roomful of angry kids, but it should be part of our long-term policy to make what we do as intelligible as possible to the people we teach. Their sense of justice may often be both passionate and crude, but we owe it both to their developing intelligence and to our own integrity to try to refine it, making clear the reasons behind actions which they may have seen as strange, unnecessary or silly. Over a period, both individual teachers and the school as a whole can establish a pattern of reasonable discussion, where complaints are listened to seriously, criticisms levelled and answered, unpopular decisions explained and justified, and obvious injustices corrected. Some imposition may still take place, since the achievement of mutual trust and respect will be neither instant nor invariable, but this apparent contradiction need not matter if the overall commitment to honesty and reason is felt to be genuine. In this, as in much else, we have to trust kids to come to the right conclusions, and they cannot come to them if we try to drag them there.

A central problem, for example, is the concept of consistency. Traditional descriptions of fairness imply that everyone is treated the same, and we have intensified the already powerful instinct of kids to demand that treatment should be fair, or identical; crime x leads to punishment y, and if criminal A gets punished and criminal B does

not, then that is 'unfair'. And so it is, but even the apparently mono-
lithic legal system does not work with quite that degree of mathematical
exactness: people who drive at 80 m.p.h. do get fined and endorsed –
unless they are rally drivers, ambulance men going to an emergency,
charming young ladies or simply individuals lucky enough not to be
caught. In the same way, a £20 fine is the same for everyone, except
that it is a crippling blow for some and for others an incidental
expense. Is that 'fair'?

In schools, this disparity is even more marked. A caning, extended
talk or letter home mean dramatically different things to different
pupils, and a tight, accurate scale of punishment is even less available
to us than it is to the law. More important still, our function is not
simply punitive, in that (unlike the courts) we retain our customers
before, during and after any offence, and therefore cannot confine
ourselves to merely penal criteria. Because we are educating as well
as punishing, caring as well as controlling, we necessarily adopt a
variety of standards. Large-scale operation implies common demands,
with the possibility of penal enforcement; books brought, movement
restricted, shouting controlled and property protected. But individual
treatment requires sensitivity, flexibility and the chance to change
routine; less pressure, an unorthodox admission or bargain, the possibility of a fresh start. Thus penal and psychological demands frequently conflict, and we cannot allow the external attractions of
standardised justice to deprive us of the power to treat different kids
differently, according to their personal circumstances and the varied
insights and experiences of their teachers or tutors.

Our fairness, therefore, is not in the vengeful equation of 'an eye
for an eye', but in the close, sympathetic attention given to each case.
The results of that attention may well vary, even for kids who may
seem to have committed very similar crimes, but the consistency will
lie in the personal consideration given to each child involved and the
common involvement in the tutorial system rather than in particular
measures adopted. This is a sophisticated distinction, which can sometimes be explained to individual kids in private but which may not be
immediately easy to grasp. It may not reassure the victim of a bully
who wants to know what has happened to his tormentor, and it
probably will not answer the irate father whose child has had a
fountain-pen stolen, but it is nonetheless the best we can do.

This unspectacular, specific approach extends also to more positive
areas. Just as our justice is necessarily relative to the individual kids
with whom we deal, so is our deliberate and increasing allowance of
freedom. Freedom, most of us would agree, is a power and a right, but

which freedoms, and for whom? When should they be offered, and how? For what reason?

Personally, I would aim to maximise my pupils' range of choice over the nature and direction of their work, although as their teacher I would retain the responsibility to supervise and comment on their progress, making suggestions and at times insisting on these being carried out. Offering choices, too, presupposes the reality of the choice offered, and in the early stages of a year, or course, or school career, it may well be necessary to impose a compulsory diet in order to prepare for subsequent choices. I would encourage pupils to initiate and run as many activities as possible (sports teams, dances, clubs, plays), with an increasing range of resources and effect as they grow older (a greater say in the use of money, a wider impact upon the local community) and a decreasing significance in the participation of staff. I would not, on the other hand, stop checking equipment, ordering books or keeping confidential records, nor would I expect pupils to punish each other or to appoint staff. Between these extremes, there are a whole range of similar decisions which I would not see as crucial (what pupils should wear, who the governors should be, how often the staff should meet) but which in some situations might well be urgent.

The same goes for trust. We need, obviously, to trust our pupils if they are going to trust us, just as we must respect them if we expect to earn respect. But what, precisely, does 'trust' mean? Abolishing registers, leaving handbags open, locking no cupboards, making homework voluntary, opening the school at all hours, not counting tools at the end of the lesson, letting kids go to the lavatory during lessons, or what? For me, trust – like discipline – is a means to an end; I trust a kid not as a reward for what he has done, but in order that he should do something, in order that our relationship should change. This means that I am still left with some tricky, borderline decisions; 'trust' is not an absolute, rescuing me from the need to make distinctions. For instance, when I have lent a kid a pen, do I ask for it back or wait for him to give it to me? If he does not, do I chase him up next day, or write it off as lost? The answers will be mine, and will rightly depend on me and the kid, but the point is that my initial choice of emphasis ('Reason, Justice, Freedom') is only the start of the journey. The important distinctions have still to be made, today, tomorrow and the day after that.

Growth

For me as a teacher thinking about my work, the crucial point is not whether what I do is right or wrong, by some static moral judgement. School is not a building or an institution, but a process, and the test of a teacher's work is not what it looks like but where it leads. When you and your kids get rid of each other, how much better or worse off are they for having suffered your attentions?

In this context, of perpetual movement and constant change (only partly at the instigation of the school), the exercise of discipline gives the teacher the time and attention to direct kids towards helpful, useful or enjoyable activities which will make that development more positive than it might otherwise have been. Sometimes kids should choose or initiate their own activity, and sometimes they will be better off for the teacher having limited the alternatives; but that very choice between self-direction and direction is itself part of the direction, the constant, daily and irrevocable prerogative of the teacher.

Insofar as freedoms are denied, it is because they are either unnecessary or destructive (the freedom to tip others off their chairs, for instance, or the freedom to do nothing), or because to deny them temporarily will enable you in time to refine a definition which might otherwise be unclear (the freedom to move around the class, or to speak freely in discussion). Discipline in this context is part of a gradual, even sporadic, development in which pupils move towards a more decisive, adult and responsible role.

This is both a valid educational aim, and incidentally a means of creating a more orderly situation. Many of the kids who currently behave in a silly, rude or destructive manner do so because their past experience of school seems to have offered them no alternative equally attractive and accessible. If we can change the very meaning of 'school' for such pupils, they will not only be wiser and more fulfilled, but also less troublesome. School should mean activity, company, co-operation, choice, challenge, interest, enjoyment, facilities, variety and achievement, and it should mean these things for all pupils. Given a different experience of school, whole pupil populations (rather than gifted individuals, or selected classes) can identify with the institution they attend, and feel the need to attack it less urgently and less often.

Changing 'what school means' is so formidable a task that it needs to be done by groups rather than individuals, schools rather than departments, communities rather than teachers. The work involved may seem strange or unnecessary, until we look at the alternative. Why should the future successors of those pupils who are currently silly, rude or destructive behave any differently *unless* we can make it worth their while? This is not a verbal contract; practically, we have to make the experience of school life and work so satisfying for kids that it is not only 'better' and wiser to behave constructively than to muck about, but also more enjoyable.

To agree on such a change is a large step for a school to take, and the mere fact of the decision will not work wonders. A 16 year old in his last year of a school career he thinks of as senseless, boring and wasteful will not be transformed by a revised curriculum. Nor will the small number of highly disturbed children be made instantly biddable and polite by a school régime which consciously seeks to extend their independence. Hard cases, however, are not the only test, and the overall gains for most pupils will create an atmosphere in which violent confrontations are both less likely and more easy for the school community to absorb.

The shared effort involved in such a change would be new for many schools, and the traditional means of public proclamation and headmasterly dictatorship would not be sufficient to achieve it. For a whole school to alter the nature of its teacher-pupil relationships, all the teachers in the school would need to be involved in the consideration, as well as the implementation, of restructuring. You cannot force people to be sensitive, positive and far-sighted.

This condition will disqualify such a scheme instantly in many minds, let alone schools. Cynics assume that 'the average teacher' is both hostile to and incapable of change, but few cynics have had the experience of working in a school which has deliberately chosen to extend its possibilities in this way. Such a change of direction, and the increasing flexibility and honesty which must accompany it, can liberate the most unexpected talents and energies, and widen the range of possible satisfactions for staff as well as kids.

We have, then, to deal simultaneously with a number of different experiences, different rhythms of growth. Just as the young teacher acquires in time the capacity to relax, experiment and take risks, so his class develops its own identity, less tense, more settled and more trusting. Individual teachers also have their own phases of development, in their relationships with individual pupils, classes and the whole school, as well as over the duration of their teaching careers. Individual kids, too, will within their time at school experience changing relationships with their peers and a variety of teachers, as well as occupying a fluid position in the life of the school. The communities of the staff-room, the pupil population (as a whole, in houses and year groups, as well as in much smaller units) and the school will each have an identity and a history: beginnings, growth, crises, innovations and so on.

The problem, and the challenge, is to synchronise these separate rhythms of growth, so that individual needs (for academic success, personal maturity, social responsibility, teacher confidence, sharing of decisions) can be met at the same time that communal exploration takes place. This cannot be charted externally on a master time-table of satisfactions, but all those who work in the school need to be aware of the simultaneous developments of which they are a part, so that the demands made by some kinds of growth ('A' level passes or social confidence for kids, career prospects or staff-room democracy for teachers) do not destroy the chances for other kinds of growth, in different areas or alternative directions. A lot of us are travelling at once, but from various starting-points towards separate destinations and at varying speeds.

Such visions of change may seem a far cry from the skirmishes of Part Two, but there is a vital connection between teacher control and eventual change, in that the main responsibility for initiating reforms must rest with the teachers. Insofar as there is a vicious circle, the teachers must break it; they have the strongest motive to alter the present pattern of relationships, the potential awareness to see the need for change and the necessary power to make a real difference. Pupils, by contrast, usually have experience of only one secondary school, and without teacher support have very little chance of affecting the pattern of their schooling, however impeccable their arguments or militant their marches.

Ultimately, of course, it becomes a kind of partnership, but in the long and difficult transition which precedes that ultimate, teachers will need to be in control. In trying to strengthen the position of the teacher, I do not argue for any moral superiority or distinctively academic status, and would not deny that some teachers have abused the power they possessed so as to damage the children they have taught, but in my experience most oppression of pupils by teachers derives from fear in the teacher; a reduction of the teacher's power, in such cases, therefore, might well lead to more cruelty and tension rather than to less.

Teachers need control *for the sake of the kids*, and a loss of teacher control is not a gain for anyone. Kids are most free where their teachers have the confidence to allow them freedom, and that confidence comes from a sense of assurance, familiarity and strength which in most schools will require some initial exercise of control. Only in the short-term heat of battle are the interests of kids and teachers opposed; in the long term, better, more secure teachers must mean freer and happier kids, which in turn means an improvement both in the narrow field of discipline and in the wider quality of education.

Such a development needs, however, to be placed within a time-scale which takes account of the human limitations of both teacher and taught. There are severe limits to what one inexperienced teacher, working alone, can achieve with classes who have never met him before, and it is for that reason that significant changes in schools will be a gradual, communal and responsible process.

It is for that reason also that a young teacher needs to fix his immediate sights on the short-term aim of survival, not as a contradiction of more positive goals but as a precondition of their achievement. Teaching can be rewarding, satisfying and genuinely exciting, but it can also – especially early on – be wearing and depressing, and in my subjective view a clear, honest study of discipline is the best way to minimise grief and encourage eventual exploration. Once the initial questions have been answered, the petty details taken care of, the atmosphere set and the systems established, then it becomes entirely possible for teacher and kids to move past the obsession with containment into a more creative relationship, out of the struggle for power, beyond control.

Index